China's last but one matriarchy

The Jino of Yunnan

Pedro Ceinos Arcones

Papers of the White Dragon, Kunming, 2013.

Papers of the White Dragon

peceinos@hotmail.com

Kunming 2013

Acknowledgements

I want to express my thanks to the people whose collaboration has been important during my field trips and to those to help in the final writing of this book. People in the villages of Baduo, Bapo and Basha were very friendly patiently explaining to me the main characteristics of Jino culture, as they were in "classical" times, and as they are lived nowadays.

I want to thank specially to the zhuoba of Bapo village, Piaoze and his family. We never forget the two Temaoke festivals we enjoyed with them. Mr Bai, expert in Jinuo dance make some interesting remarks during our brief interview.

I want to express my thanks to Miss Che Jiabei to allow me to use her picture in the front page of my book.

In Kunming, Li Quanming reviewed my final draft, and Emma Milligan and Florence Rountree checked my English to make this book easily readable. To all them and those I could have forget, my sincere thanks.

Contents

Preface: The wonderful culture of the Jino

Hidden in the tropical mountains of China's southern border lives one of the most interesting Chinese minorities: The Jino nationality. With a population of only 21,000 people they are one of the less known ethnic groups in China, who in the past were often confused with the surrounding minorities. The study of their culture started only in the last decades of the 20th century and showed the world an ethnic group characterized for the strength with which they preserved their matriarchal tendencies and their surprising adaptability to their tropical environment.

The Jino inhabit a cluster of villages dispersed along the mountainous forest of the final Chinese section of the Mekong basin. In this sometimes impenetrable succession of mountains, a complex environment where survival has been always difficult, the Jino developed throughout the centuries a sophisticated culture that allowed them to make sustainable use of the limited resources available.

The Jino are the last of the national minorities officially recognized by the Chinese government. Before 1979, when their ethnic status was granted, they were considered to be Dai, Hani or Yi, depending on the areas where they lived. When Chinese anthropologists began to study the main characteristics of the Jino culture, they discovered to their surprise that the Jino had many traces of a past matriarchal society, only recently disappeared, and it was also found that they lived in villages where the land was a common property worked on together by all the villagers and whose fruits were shared equitably, similar to the game caught on their hunting expeditions.

The shadow of their former matriarchy, and of their goddesses, was found everywhere in the Jino life and culture, as a giant umbrella that covered their main activities, especially prominent in their myths and legends, as well as in the spiritual life that directed their everyday activities: farming and hunting, house building, village ceremonies and rituals performed by their main religious specialists.

The apparent simplicity of this original society slowly revealed a complex technology developed by hundreds of years of adaptation to their particular environment, a technology that allowed them to continuously inhabit lands that otherwise would have been fit for habitation only for a short time. At the heart of this technology was a reverential respect for the mother earth, embodied especially as the Goddess of the Fields and the Lady of the Beasts, and a common exhaustive knowledge of the different kinds of soils, their responses to the changing climatic conditions, to the seasonal weather oscillations, and to different rice varieties. Their ideas about the characteristics of their soils basically correspond with modern geological classifications; their calendar of 11 months (designed to remember the main steps in the creation process of the goddess Amoyaobai) fits perfectly with their agricultural activities; their knowledge of more than 100 varieties of rice allowed them to optimally use every natural resource.

The organization of labor along the seasons was designed to allow the maximum yield for the agriculture, fish and hunting in a sustainable way that preserved the ecological systems of their territory. They were complemented by the complex gathering of roots, tubers, plants, fruits and flowers, bamboos and mushrooms, reaching several hundred kinds of vegetable species, of which different parts were used for specific purposes and were extracted with original technological processes.

The Jino are one of the most complex chapters in the history of the adaptation of humankind to the natural environment. Their culture provides a master lesson of sustainable economy. Their main features, the cult of the great goddesses and of the wood drum that symbolizes the soul of the village, lead us to a primitive duality in which human beings became the central axis in the relationship between the all-powerful heaven and earth.

Duality permeates all the religious and social concepts of the Jino; they consider themselves to be the product of the marriage of two mythic siblings that survived the flood floating inside a big wooden drum: brother Mahei and sister Maniu. Their descendants divided themselves to inhabit matriarchal and patriarchal villages, a concept still alive nowadays, as most of the villages are composed of families that belong to two exogamous clans, whose members cannot marry inside the clan. Villages are governed by the two eldest people of each of these clans, the zhuoba or the mother of the village from the first clan that established the village, and the zhuosheng or father of the village, representing the second clan. Each of them keeps in his house a wooden drum, a reminder of the way the ancestors of the Jino survived the great flood, the mother drum placed before the house of the "mother of the village" and the father drum before the house of the "father".

11

This system of government of the villages is one of the most democratic known in the anthropological register as each person will suffice to live as long as is needed to become a leader. His rule is aided with the assistance provided by a council of elders and neighborhood organizations where groups of families are responsible for different communal tasks.

The psychological adaptation made necessary by the imposing nature where the Jino live, caused them to develop original concepts, including respecting nature as a mother through impersonating numerous goddesses and feminine deities, the ritual marriage between the Jino spiritual leaders and these goddesses, to provided them with some powers, and the care kept along the whole productive process to not destroy the spiritual balance between humans and nature, in a way that even the capture of a small bamboo rat or a little bird was accompanied by the corresponding ritual to thank the incumbent goddess. This concept of the universe based on the balance between humans and nature, is also reflected in their material culture, where villages, houses and even people's clothes contain symbols of this cosmic integration.

The Jino have preserved a ritual cycle that reflects the yearly natural cycle and humans' adaptation to it. During their two main festivals, Temaoke, a happy homage to the blacksmith who provides them with the tools needed for agriculture at the beginning of the year, and Luomaluo, the sad mourning for the death of the Great Goddess Amoyaobai, life and death succeed each other as part of a cosmic cycle common to all natural beings.

Nowadays the primitive agricultural system that for centuries sustained the simple lives of generations of the Jino people is quickly transforming so that economic crops are given priority. Rubber, tea, banana and other fruits and ornamental trees are found everywhere, and with them the promise of a possibly richer future for the Jino. A future, however, full of challenges in which their wellbeing will not rely anymore in their perfect knowledge of their natural environment but in the fluctuations of markets that they neither understand nor are able to control.

This book is the first comprehensive introduction to the Jino life and culture published in English. In the following pages we will try to give the reader a general idea of the main characteristics of the Jino's lifestyles, culture, religion and history. To do it we have divided the book in eight chapters. The first, *General aspects of Jino culture*, is a basic introduction to the Jino name, geographical localization, natural environment, languages and dialects, with a special mention of their alternate signs languages, and Jino ethnic branches. The second chapter is about *Jino history*, from their mythic account of creation by the Great Goddess to the establishing of their main branches by powerful shamanesses, and the account of the process that changed their society from matriarchal to patriarchal. Special emphasis has been put on trying to relate their mythic account to a workable old history of the Jino. The third chapter, *Jino Religion*, introduces their main beliefs, deities (most goddesses), religious specialists and rituals. The fourth chapter is about the *Jino Life Cycle*, their ideas about birth, rites of passages, marriage ways and funeral customs are described, and the matriarchal tracts in Jino culture fully exposed. The fifth chapter contains a description of the main festivals of the Jino, especially the Luomaluo and Temaoke festivals. The sixth chapter *Material Culture of the Jino* describes their economic activities, with special attention paid to their complex agricultural system and the structure and symbolism of their villages, houses and clothes. The seventh, *Intangible culture of the Jino*, provides the

13

reader a short introduction of their main myths and legends, song and dances, and the symbolism of their wooden drum. In the eighth, *Contemporary life of the Jino*, we outline the changes that the last decades brought to the Jino life and culture. In the appendix we provide the first translation of their creation myth: *Goddess Amoyaobai created the world.*

Approximate location of the Jino.

(Adapted from "National Minorities of China" map, in LL-MAP. Language and location. www.llmap.org/images/LanguageAtlasChina/NationalMinorities.jpg)

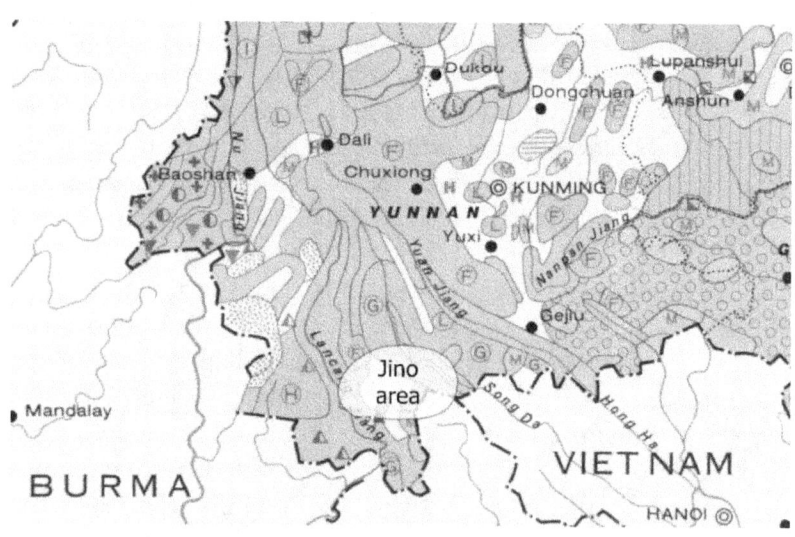

Chapter 1

General aspects of Jino culture

Name and localization

The Jino, with a population of only 21.500 persons (in 2005) are one of the smallest minorities in China and the last to be officially recognized as such, as they were designated a national minority and granted the special rights allowed by this title only in June 1979, when the State Council considered that their own spoken (but not written) language, customs, culture, economic system, and psychological environment are not shared with other peoples (Zhong 1983: 25; Zhi 1984: 86).

They were formerly known as Youle, for the name of the mountains they inhabit, but after their official recognition both them and the mountains were changed to Jino, the name they call themselves, and their territory called Jinolok. The name Youle (a deformation of the Chinese *diaole* "lost") makes reference to the legends that say that they originated in the third century from a group of Zhuge Liang soldiers that overslept and remained lost from the main body of the army. We will study in more detail this legend in the history section.

Regarding the name "Jino" there are two alternate explanations. Some authors say that in their language "ji" means maternal uncle, and "nuo" means "coming next". So

15

"Jinuo" would mean "descendants of the uncle", a reference that suggests in the near past they lived in a matriarchal society. The maternal uncle, the main man in a family ruled by a woman, is very important in matriarchal societies and the persistence of the uncles' power in the family and society life indicates that in the past family power was shared by sister and brother and not between wife and husband.

Even today the uncle holds a very important role in each Jino life. He acts as protagonist in child naming ceremonies, betrothal and marriages; he even has the power to approve a marriage even if it is prevented by the couple's parents (Bai and Zhang 2000: 32). As a protector of his nephew or niece he can take care of children born before marriage, and assist his nephews in case of weakness and sickness, tying a red string in their wrist to protect them and even chewing the food that they will eat when they feel weak. Others consider that "ji" means crowded and "nuo" means behind, being a reference to the moment when Jino and other peoples came out of the gourd in disorder in mythical times (Zhao 1995: 4).

The Jino only have about 1,300 families, inhabiting about 40 villages (most of them moved in the last years to more accessible localizations) scattered over 3,000 square kilometers up in the mountains (Zhi 1984: 86). Their administrative center is Jinoshan Township, a cluster of new houses and administrative buildings in the most accessible part of Jino territory, which lies only 100 km away from Laos's border. It belongs to the Jinghong Municipality in the Xishuangbanna Dai Autonomous Prefecture, Yunnan Province.

Natural environment

Jino Mountain, an area of roughly 70 km from east to west and 50 km from north to south (Du and Yip 1993: 224), constitutes the main territory of Jino minority; a region of subtropical weather with seasonal raining in the wet season, and an abundance of endemic animal and vegetal species. Near the Jino can be found some Yi, Hani and Kongge (one of the not yet officially recognized Chinese ethnic groups) communities, and in the lowlands around them, with different branches of Dai peoples. The northern limit of Jino territory is defined by a valley into which the Nanxiaohe and Xiaoheijiang rivers flow. On the south, west and east it borders Mengyang, Jinghong, Menghan, and the Menglun basin in Mengla County. The Mekong and the Xiaoheijiang rivers meander through this basin and they meet right at the foot of the Jino mountains (Yin 2001: 216). The elevation of Jino mountains ranges from 1,691 meter in the highest point to 550 meter in the lowest. Temperature is pleasant, as the hot weather of tropical Xishuangbanna is cooled by the mountains environment. It ranges from 34.9°C to 5.8°C, with an annual average of 18-20°C. The rainfall amount is 1,580,5 millimeters each year. There are only two seasons in the year: raining season from May to September and a dry season for the other months (Lu and Kang 2006). Jino Mountain is rich in biodiversity and mineral resources. Forests cover 67.7% of Jino area, including the tropical rain forest and subtropical green foliage forest. More than 1,000 kinds of trees and 2,000 kinds of plants of economic value are found in these forests. Jino mountains are rich in wildlife; they are the home to more than 100 species of mammals, 36 amphibians, 60 reptiles, 420 birds and 100 fishs, including elephants, wild oxen and a variety of monkeys (Lu and Kang 2006). The biggest elephant's natural reserve in Xishuangbanna is situated just on the border of Jino territory.

These exuberant natural resources allowed the Jino to survive practicing shifting cultivation, gathering non-timber forest products, hunting and fishing for their livelihood. To get their maximum yields sustainably they developed a unique system through the knowledge of their natural resources and the environment, including the economic value of 252 botanical species (Wang).

Language and dialects

Jino language belongs to the Sino-Tibetan family, Tibetan-Burman branch, Yi or Loloish sub-branch. That means that we can expect to find some cultural similarities between the Jino and other ethnic groups speaking related languages, such as the Yi, Naxi, Lahu, Hani or Lisu, etc. While they have kept some cultural tracts that relate them with the mainstream of the Loloish languages, their folkways resemble that of their neighbors Hani-Akha, with whom they were sometimes confused with in the past (Ramsey 1987: 264). Their language structure however seems very similar to the Burmish sub-branch of the Tibeto-Burman languages (Hayasi 2009: 256). Like other Tibeto-Burman ethnic groups, it is supposed that the Jino migrated from the northwest of Yunnan province to their present territories, but the timing and routes of this migration remain uncertain.

Jino language has two main dialects, namely Youle or proper Jino and Buyuan. Youle dialect is spoken in the core territory of the Jino, in Jino Mountain, by about 90% of the Jino population; Buyuan dialect, however, is spoken only by between 1,000 and 3,000 Jino living in the more isolated communities in Buyuan Mountain to the north of Jino Township (Gai 1986: 255). The linguistic James Matisoff (2003:747) considers that there are five different sub-groupings

18

of the Jino language: Baka, Banai, Baya, Buyuan, and Youle. The differences between the dialects are big, especially with regards to vocabulary, keeping more similitude in grammatical structure. Usually it is difficult for people speaking one dialect to understand Jino who are speaking other dialect.

The language usage among the Jino is rapidly decreasing. In the 1980s it was estimated that about seventy or eighty percent of the population could speak Jino (Gai 1986: 255), while in the first years of the 21st century it is possible that fewer than half of the total population can speak the language. Although it seems that in some areas most of the young Jino cannot speak their native language and even Brenzinge (2007: 288), states that: "I never met a young Jinuo who can speak the language, despite years of trying" in our visits to Jino territory we found that Jino is becoming the home language, where it is exclusively used and Chinese is the language used to communicate with the outside world.

Jino language is complex, Youle dialect has 35 initial consonants and 16 vowels, and between 6 and 8 tones, depending of the areas as there are important variations between the language of different villages (Yu 2000: 77). It can be characterized by its complex tone *sandhi* (a feature of tonal languages in which the tones assigned to individual words vary based on the pronunciation of the words that surround them) and for its conservatism with initial consonants. The order of the sentence is: subject - object - predicate. They have many borrowed words from the Dai and the Chinese (Song 2007: 296). The Buyuan dialect has 30 initial consonants and 27 vowels (Yu 2000: 80).

Alternate languages

19

Not having a writing system, the Jino developed several systems of signs that covered communication in different situations: from the wooden gates in the mountain paths that warn of danger, to the *daliu* to expel demons, the wooden swords at the edges of the fields to mark one's territory, the compositions of leaves to express their love, or the engraved boards and bamboos to record debts (Yu 2000: 82)

Engraved wooden or bamboo boards to record debts and economic interchanges reached a great complexity among the Jino. In the past each Jino village had eight boards where a general account of the village grains, meat, horses, etc. were engraved. Every head of the family had at the head of his bed seven small boards where there were carved systems of small and big cuts to record their debts with the village (Yu 2000). After carving the big and small cuts on a board, it was separated into two parts that were kept respectively by the head of the village and the head of the family. Each account has one woodcut. Every time the money was handed in, they will make a mark on the woodcut. When the debt was completely paid they checked carefully to be sure that the two segments of the board fixed well and the board was then broken (MSD). To avoid confusion sometimes they added something related to the nature of the debt, such grains of rice or corn or cotton flowers to indicate that rice, corn or cotton was lent, carefully glued to the board to avoid the danger of rats eating it.

Just before the modern reforms of the 1950s the system of carving boards was so well developed that one person in the villages had the duty to supervise this process and to update yearly the villager's accounts. Sometimes they also used real items to count, with grains of rice or corn representing units of a determined product or service, but it was a cumbersome method in which it was easy to make mistakes, and not as developed as the carving system (Jino 1999: 42).

There is another set of symbols, some of them chosen by analogy, that have a definite meaning for the Jino people, such as the bronze bracelet that the husband gives his wife on the wedding, which symbolizes the permanency expected in the marriage; or chicken feathers, that are symbols of happiness as they announce the arrival of a new day. The crest of the chicken is a symbol of health for its healthy color. Hanging things in the earlobe is a symbol of laboriousness. "When a messenger delivered an urgent verbal message he carried a red pepper to show that it was an important matter, a piece of burning coal symbolizing a torch and a chicken feather to indicate urgency" (Zhi 1984: 92; Yu 2000:86).

There are other symbols with religious meaning used in their ceremonies or to keep away evil spirits, such as the *daliu* structures, or village gates, etc. Every village had a human gravure of wood to protect against fire and every 5 to 7 houses a smaller one, also supposed to protect against fire and theft.

Lovers used leaves letters to express their feelings, which were usually hung on the road or crossroads for the loved one. One of the most popular designs consisted of two bundles of leaves tied up together in human shape with a red string. The leaves can wither but the red string can not, meaning that the love between these persons would never wither and will live forever (Yu 2000: 82).

Branches

The Jino nationality can be divided into three branches, Axi, Aha and Wuyou, each with their own characteristics.

According to their legends the three branches were founded by three ancestral mothers worshipped during their most important ceremonies, which divided their homes and, from then on, their offspring. The Axi branch (whose main villages are Baya, Badou, Baxiu, Huilu, Huizheng, Base, Balai, Buxi) and the Aha branch (whose main villages are Zuoke, Zuolei, Babo, Lete, Bagui, Pumi, Babie, Baka) live in the southern part of the Jino territory. Their villages are near each other and their culture blends into a unified Jino culture, although there are still differences in folkways, religion, language and dress.

The people who belong to the Wuyou branch live in the northern part of Jino Mountain. Although there are some isolated Jino communities still deep in the forest, whose history and culture has not been properly researched; most of the Wuyou villages moved in 2002 to more accessible locations near the Mengwang Township. The language (almost unintelligible to the other Jinos), culture, dress and even festivals seem to be different from the other two branches. The women's dress follows the same pattern but with some colors added. Houses are not different. Local leaders say they are about 3,000 people. Their culture has been influenced by the Han instead of the Dai. Wuyou branch only started to celebrate Temaoke Festival (the most important for the other branches) until recently, under the Jino Mountain influence and the government's inclusion of all them as one nationality, but they celebrate it later, about February 13th (Zhu 2009: 8).

Chapter 2

History of the Jino

Although nowadays Jino nationality is a present cultural construction whose existence does not implies its extension in the history to a hypothetical moment of ethnic birth somehow related to their original myths, a line in the time could be draw back, tying up with it different historically (imagined or real) situations with which the Jino people identify themselves. In this chapter we will try to arrange some of these situations in an intelligible historical or figurate order perhaps that allows them to be comprehensible to the modern reader.

History teaches us that present day Chinese minorities were built through centuries of interaction between peoples of different stocks. In the case of the Jino early Tibeto-Burman cultural influences possibly from Northwest Yunnan, early Chinese influences, Austronesic life ways maybe or original populations of Jino Mountains, or acquired by the Jino as adaptation to the tropical environment, as well as later (post 18th century) Tibeto-Burman (Yi, Hani-Akha), Chinese and Dai influences can be found.

Mother goddess creates the world - Mythical history.

While the mythical narrative *Amoyaobai* provides a comprehensive historical account of the creation of the world, human beings and of the first steps of men on earth, it is difficult to consider the facts described in the narration as historical facts. In the Amoyaobai myth the goddess appeared in an empty world and with her inexhaustible force she created earth, with plains, valleys and mountains. She created animals and plants to feed human beings and at the end she created human beings.

With the products of her creation she established a kind of ecological balance where each animal was controlled, placing human beings at the top of this world. Human beings, originally situated amid the rest of the animals, were constantly favored by the goddess, who taught them how to avoid the dangerous attacks of the wild animals, how to control them and how to survive the disasters of the seven suns and of a protracted darkness. At the end Amoyaobai divided the human beings in Han, Dai and Jino, and summoned them to share the goods of her creation, but as the Jino lived far they arrived late to the call of the goddess receiving only the worst lands and cultural implements. In this way the main characteristics of these three ethnic groups were established. At the end Amoyaobai died and the Jino mourned her for 13 days, remembered every year in the Luomaluo Festival.

The origin of make offerings to the ancestors is the second part of the Jino mythic history. It tells how one day the waters began to rise and a terrible flooding took place. To survive the disaster the brother and sister Mahei and Maniu made a wooden drum hollowing a tree trunk and covering its two ends with cowhides. After many days the twins drifted in the waters until their drum landed again on dry land. After being sure that they were the only humans being left on the earth they married each

24

other to recreate the humankind. Surprisingly the new humanity was not born directly from them, but from a giant gourd that grew from the only gourd-seed that survived the flood. The coming out of the new humanity was possible only after the ancestor Apierer sacrificed her body to let the people out of the gourd.

After the creation of this new humankind, the comprehensive linear logic of the mythic narration contrasts with the apparently contradictory statements that we find in the Jino legends which try to explain their history. Some legends say that after leaving the drum Maniu and Mahei gave birth to seven boys and seven girls who later married each other giving origin to the Jino people, other legends state that they had only seven children, the eldest was bitten and killed by a wasp, the other six made three couples that gave origin to the three branches of the Jino. It must be noted that in both legends the number seven, powerful lunar and feminine symbol, is present. Of the seven children of Mahei and Maniu, the two elders married and gave origin to the Wuyou branch whose name means "twig of the tree", the two second eldest created the Aha (tree forks) branch, and the two youngest created the Axi (tree sprouts) branch (Outlook 1999: 56)

Trying to reconstruct a kind of historical framework from these legends with such contradictory information sometimes contradictory we assumed that the Jino history contained the following situations.

1. Migration to present lands. Though some researches affirm that the Jino were the original inhabitants of the Jino Mountains, nobody denies that they arrive there from another place. Jino legends relate that they migrated from an ancestral home further north, maybe in Pu'er, Mojiang or even further,

25

to the Jino Mountains. The path that their shamans follow when they lead the dead souls to the ancestors' lands ends in Jino Mountain. Yet linguistic and cultural reasons suggest that they come from the northwest of Yunnan province. It seems likely that they still lived in a matriarchal society when they first settled around the Jino Mountain. This long migration from Northwest Yunnan helps to understand their language and cultural links with other Loloish groups, and their early presence in Jino Mountain.

2. Sijiezhuomi. All the Jino consider Sijiezhuomi as a sacred mountain where they arrived. Sijiezhuomi is also the mythical post-flood time when they experienced their first social development. At this time they had consanguineous marriage. Legend has it that the first settler on the mountain ridge was a widow by the name of Jiezhou. The name of the first village Jiezhou, suggest it was established by an ancestral mother. We will see that Jiezhou is in other narrations the next step in social development. As the population grew, the big family was divided into two groups, two clans that could intermarry. Sijiezhuomi is still the place where they send the souls of the dead people, which it is possibly situated around Simao. The study of the Naxi after-death beliefs suggest that rituals of sending the soul to the ancestors' lands are part of the patriarchal cluster of beliefs. The fact that the Jino send their souls to Sijiezhuomi point out that their patriarchal tendencies surged after they were established in Jino Mountain (Ceinos 2012). Other post death sacred land, which seems more related with matriarchal society, is the sacred land of Tailuomengmo.

Tailuomengmo is the mythical land where their main goddesses have their villages and where the goddess Beimo stores the children that will be born. The bailabao travels to this mythical land in the ceremonies to get the new born children. The souls of deceased bailabao, beimo and blacksmith are also supposed to come here. This is also the place from where the ritual specialists get their magic skills in their ceremonies as it is also the villages of their respective goddesses (Outlook 1999). This is a kind of sacred Kingdom of Goddesses from where all life comes. It is well known that shamans must keep the traditions that guarantee their powers, it is possible that this land was older than the place where nowadays the souls of the dead are sent, so the matriarchal realm is older that the patriarchal one.

3. Two moieties. The group on the mountain-face was patriarchal and the group on the rear slope matriarchal (with evident connections to the yin-yang theory whose first and original meaning refers to the sunny (yang) and shadowy (yin) faces of a mountain). They lived in mountain ridges and used tree leaves and animal skins as clothing and led a hard life of hunting and food gathering (Du and Yip 1993: 224). Afterwards, the group on the mountain-face fragmented into a patriarchal village called Citong and a matriarchal one called Manduo. The group on the rear slopes also divided into two groups. From this we can see that the earliest Jino settlements were probably two clans which had split from a moiety and then produced the ten or so daughter clans. This suggests that in ancient times the Jino passed through a matriarchal commune stage and probably also a stage of primitive communism in which between five and twenty families lived in a single long-house (Zhu 1989).

4. Jiezhou times. After leaving Sijiezhuomi the three Jino branches separated, it is said that the Wuyou people delayed eating crabs and later they were not able to find the other branches. Then while Wuyou branch moved to the east while the Aha and Axi went on to the southwest, to Jiezhou, another mythic mountain about 60 km away from today Jino Township

27

(Yu 2000: 5). Only some Wuyou arrived to Jizhou but the whole Aha and Axi people did. Now all of them send their soul to Sijiezhuomi but the soul's road of the Wuyou branch does not include Jiezhou Mt. The name Jiezhou can be translated as "the place where the human beings became clever", because in the time they lived there they experienced important changes in marriage customs, production lives and social organization. In Jiezhou they developed the concept of the village god (Sijie Asi) inhabiting the wooden drum in which Mahei and Maniu survived the flood, and the idea that they must keep two wooden drums in each village: one male, smaller with the spirit of Mahei inside and one bigger, female, with the spirit of Maniu. At this time they still lived as hunter-gatherers, but as the population increased the game and edible foods became scarcer; they started their slash and burn agriculture and husbandry (Yu 2000: 17). In Jiezhou they have bigger and better villages, agriculture surged, trade developed, and they started the Temaoke festival to the blacksmith. There are legends about the presence of foreign peoples being among them. Consanguineous marriages were forbidden. Zhuoba and zhuosheng leaders surged in this time and were carried by women, called zhoumi youke, "the venerated grandma that loves people".

At this time humans and spirits were not separated; after death humans became spirits, who usually came back home, where they eat and sleep, and if the people didn't feed them, they would in turn disturb their lives. With the passing of time there were more and more dead people to feed, and as they were dead they cannot work, this put a growing pressure on their living descendants. However an old couple discovered that *daliu* and ginger kept the spirits away, and humans and spirits were separated. After that they put two big stones at the gate of the village, and gave a great feast to the spirits declaring that

28

it was the last time they feed them and that, as long as the stones stand spirits must not enter the village or they will be forced to eat ginger or count the holes of a *daliu*.

After the separation between humans and spirits the three branches of the Jino separated also, leaving the old village with the spirits of their ancestors. Then the natural territory was also separated, the village to the humans, the outside (forest, mountains, rivers and lakes) to the spirits. When people go to hunt, gather or crop, they enter the realm of the spirits and must carry on the appropriate ceremonies. In the village there is a bamboo gate with bamboo swords that means that the spirits can't enter inside (Yu 2000: 17).

In the last decades of Jiezhou Mountain, because of war with other peoples, some villages started male leadership and established new villages. Leaving Jiezhou Mt they performed the ceremony of shooting arrows at oxen, which is remembered even today when they raise a new house. Aha and Axi branches that have lived together in Jiezhou, separated and left this mountain. Axi branch moved southwest; they consider the shamaness Milijide as their ancestor. She established Situ village as a mother village and later the father village of Baduo. People from the parents' villages intermarried creating new villages, most of them in the front half of Jino Mountain. Aha branch moved to the west; they consider Menbushade their ancestral mother, which established also a mother (Bapiao) and a father village (Bapu), occupying the back half of the mountain. Every year when the Luomaluo Festival takes place, people from the children villages must go to worship the goddess Amoyaobai in the mother village, in a ceremony also called Worship the Big Dragon[1]. Every three years,

---

[1] Among the Hani there is also a festival initially established to worship the goddess Amadu which ended being a feast to worship the dragon that

representatives of the parents villages visit the children villages, whose inhabitants would go to the road to welcome them (Cheng Ping 1993). Wuyou branch migrated north, to Qiema village (Yu 2000: 23).

A Matriarchal tribe pairs with Zhuge Liang soldiers

Another set of legends are related to Zhuge Liang, the famous Chinese general, philosopher and strategist who in the third century commanded an expedition to Yunnan. Zhege Liang wanted to get the allegiance of the aboriginal populations of this province to the Shu Kingdom, which established in Sichuan province, was at war with the Wei and Wu kingdoms that controlled East China. As the legends say the troops of Zhuge Liang passed through the area and set their barracks up in the mountains. When the moment of leave arrived it is said that some of the soldiers were so tired from the months of fighting and marching that they didn't hear the army call and remained sleeping. When they woke up they found that the main body of the army was now out of reach at the other side of the big river, from where Zhuge Liang, instructed them to grow tea and cotton and to build houses in the shape of his hat (Zhi 1984: 87; Cheng Ping 1993: 2).

This is a nice tale, but it has two problems. First, it is impossible for a group of soldiers to be the ancestors of a family or people without the cooperation of the (local) women. Second, the route followed by Zhuge Liang lies far away from Jino Mountain, Simao and Mojiang, being in the western and central part of Yunnan Province. These two contradictions in

---

protects the village.

Zhuge Liang legends quickly disappear if we put Jino old history in the place their language and culture point out.

If the Jino migrated not just from Puer or Mojiang, but from northwest Yunnan or the Yunnan- Sichuan border the legends seem to fit better. First, because this is the place where the Yi sub-branch of the Tibeto-Burman family of languages was spoken 2000 years ago, and was also the place where many traditions of the Yi related peoples, now shared with the Jino, existed. Second, because in this area the most powerful matriarchal tendencies are found. It is the home of the Moso matriarchal tribe, as well as of the Naxi, Yi, Pumi and Taluo, that even today show strong matriarchal tendencies, and even in Marco Polo's time (14th century) it was an area where the women took lovers at will.

In these lands they may have been in contact with the soldiers of Zhuge Liang. This fact fits well with different Jino traditions, (their migration from the north and their relation with Zhuge Liang) and also with posses a language that belongs to the Tibetan Burman family, as well as the matriarchal traces in their culture, being matriarchal tendencies especially conspicuous in this area.

If we think that in those times the Jino kept a matriarchal social structure, maybe something as that of the Moso in the 20th century, and that they showed a preference to receive the foreigners as lovers, the traditions mentioned in this area in the books of Marco Polo and the ethnological reports about the Moso, we can think that some of Zhuge Liang soldiers used to leave their camps to spend the night with the Jino women. When the time of departure arrived they preferred to remain with the women than to follow the war with their general.

It seems that the Jino are a Tibetan Burman matriarchal tribe which paired with a group of Zhuge Liang soldiers. After that the new ethnic group that had been formed left these lands and migrated south. They would keep both strong cultural influences of the Han dynasty Chinese culture, as well as their matriarchal structure during their migrations, arriving in the Jino Mountains around the 13th century.

Matriarchal society

There are many facts that suggest that the Jino lived in a matriarchal society during most of their history, and that they still lived in a matriarchal society when they arrived in Jino Mountains. Besides their mythical account of the creation that situated the goddess in the center of their world and the matriarchal hypothesis that gives sense to Zhuge Liang legends, the first narratives that could be considered to have historical basis also put the women as leaders of their communities.

Each of the three Jino branches was led in mythic-historical times by an ancestral mother. Milijide, the ancestral mother of the Axi clan, is credited by establishing Situ village and giving names to mountains and valleys. As classical cultural heroes she knew where to find animals and taught the people to hunt and to gather edible herbs. She was considered a daughter of the Goddess of the Earth, she was the first shamaness with the ability to travel underground and to change the day into night and the clever inventor that for the first time used bamboo tubes to bring water from the mountain springs, and stone to sharpen knives. She was the heroine that, in the middle of an invasion, risked her life by returning to the village to recover the sacred tripod needed for their ritual life.

Menbushade, whose name can be translated as "the fore-mother without father" was the ancestral mother of the Aha clan. She was also an inventor, priestess and protector of the sacred objects of the clan, especially the tripod, who is veneered in their main festivals, and she established their first matriarchal village. "In the past all the clan leaders were women. They were the wisest shamans; they can divine and tell enchantments, they invented the stone knife, domesticated plants, and clothes…They were not goddesses but human beings as we" (Cheng 1993: 5). Political and religious power blended in these first shamans that led the society not only because the role of women as farmers and gatherers was more important than that of men as hunters, but for their ability to provide wellbeing to the people. The title they carried would be translated as "the elders that receive the respect of the people" (Zhao 1995: 24). The origin of political power in East Asia seems to be closely linked with the leadership exerted by female shamans. Sarah Nelson (2008) provides many instances when the origin of the big kingdoms and empires or East Asia is linked to the power of female shamans. In *Matriarchy in China*, some instances of political power in the hands of shamanesses are also provided (Ceinos 2011).

Most of the Jino villages were established by feminine ancestors, and up until today the oldest woman is called Amo or mother of the village, and consanguineous marriages were common in the past (Cheng Ping 1993: 3). The circumstances which led to the establishing of the village is remembered in some villages' name, as Badou or "the place where we stopped because mother's breast ached", Babou or "the village built by our foremother", Bagui or "the village inhabited by the young women without fathers", Shaoniu or "the village of girls without fathers" as legends say it was established by a girl who

33

has no father, Aema or "the low village of the women without fathers" (Zhao 1995).

The female leadership in Jino society permeated the main aspects of their religion, culture and everyday life. The leaders of the village would be called "mothers", or even youka or grandmother in some places, even when their gender changed in an unknown historical moment. These mothers will be assisted by a council of seven members (the feminine number among the Jino and other cultures). Shamans and witches are able to get their powers only thanks to their relationship with goddesses. Their everyday life is adjusted by a horoscope of 12 signs that reflects the creation in their founding myth. The first sign is water, from where Amoyaobai surged, the second is Amoyaobai. After which came the products of her creation: the sun, moon, stars, the place where heaven and earth gather, herbs, wind, tree, rain, seven suns, and fire. Their family appellations that regard age and no gender highlight the time of consanguineous marriage.

When they build a new house, the ceremony of carrying the first fire is performed by an old woman 70 or 80 years old. She must carry a broom in one hand and a torch in the other. After putting the three stones that would make the hearth and light the fire, she must wipe the evil spirits out with the broom, so the family can enter their new house. In the banquet that follows she will be thanked with the best part of the cow offered to the spirits. In the old dances before the big drum, when women danced outside a circle of men, a *youka* leader, dressed as a woman, must enter the inner circle to dance as homage to the drum, as if the highest ritual position could only be held by women. Jiekaxi was other revered ancestress that taught them to distinguish edible plants (Wang 2004: 35)

34

If we try to frame Jino tribal history, a history in which time is not important because all the facts happened in a blurred mythical past, in the scarce chronicles about this area, it is important to acknowledge an expedition launched by the Mongols of the Yuan dynasty in the last years of the 13th century against the so called "Kingdom of the 800 maids." Almost nothing is known about this kingdom or its hypothetical situation, but due to the fact that the Mongols traveled through this area in their way to conquer Burma and the Jino could be one (maybe not the only) of the matriarchal societies there, it is possible that these Kingdom of the 800 maids referred to vague news received by the Mongol generals about matriarchal peoples living beyond the mountains through which they opened their way. It is possible that one of the foreign invaders of the Jino legends were the Mongol army. Are they the foreign invaders that forced one of the Jino southward migrations? Or the starting point in their patriarchal takeover? For the moment it is impossible to answer these questions.

Change to a patriarchal society

The Jino have several myths that narrate how the matriarchal society was transformed into a patriarchal one, transition that the experts consider happened about 300 years ago. Maybe it was a result of the arrival of iron tools and weapons and the militarization of part of the male society. According to their traditions the man who established the first patriarchal system was Apu Shalei, or Grandpa Shalei (Apu Shaxue in other records, maybe of other Jino branches); whose history is recorded in the myth *Apu Shalei has no father*. Shalei was famous for his hatred of women. The origin of this hatred it is said to have started because as he was so large he usually cannot be satisfied when the food was shared on an equal basis, as was done according to the customary law of the Jino, and suffered from hunger. His hunger turned into anger. Not being satisfied with the matriarchal society, he considered himself an enemy of women. One day when they suffered a foreign invasion, he led the young men to fight the invaders and expelled them from the Jino territory. He became a hero that won the respect of the people. On the way back to the village he wanted to kill all the women, but the warm welcome they give the warriors changed his mind, and instead, as the old village had been burnt, he established a new village, Baya, the first patriarchal village. But his thirst of blood could not be satisfied, and because of his cruel character and the continuous punishment that he inflicted on women, they planned to kill him. The knife used to kill him and the stone used to sharpen it, became sacred objects for the Jino.

After this time Jino society slowly changed. Women began to occupy a subordinate position, with the head of the family being male, and names were formed following the name of the father, women marrying outside their family, a more lenient consideration to the male sexual infidelity, and a main role of men in some rituals (Cheng 1993: 13). The appropriation for the men of the feminine roles is manifested in the names and ritual roles, continuous reference to the goddess or the instances of men dressing as women. As in the New Year Festival, when some elders narrate the Jino history and migrations while others dance and sing around the sacred drum. "Women can only dance in the outer circle, but a man dressed as a woman dance in the male circle. A vestige of the way men substituted women not only in the political and economic activities, but also on the ritual level" (Cheng 1993).

Their former matriarchal society kept, however, some of its main characteristics until 1950s, when they still had ancestors,

36

name and foremothers in common, as well as cemetery, cult and ceremonies related to the same ancestress, and after divorce, women can take with them their property and their children, and when the children get sick, only the mothers can sacrifice to the spirits to call their soul (Du 1989).

As in the history of many Chinese minorities we find many instances when the arrival of the Chinese culture put an end to their equalitarian matriarchal societies, it should not be surprising to find that one of the Chinese minorities which has preserved most matriarchal tracts until the present, was just one of the most isolated, as the Jino, living in the semi-independent Kingdom of Xishuangbanna, did not receive many Chinese influences before 1949. It is possible that the transformation of the Jino society was related to the increasing presence of Chinese tea traders in the area, whose presence supposed a hidden threat to the Jino women, and an increase of violence in the area, as the episode from the Chinese chronicles below suggests.

If the experts date the patriarchal transformation of the Jino society to have occurred around 300 years ago, we will see that it coincided with a tumultuous period in regional history, that must be framed in the efforts of the emperor Yongzheng to obtain an effective control of the border and minority regions, which led Chinese traders and migrants to an increasing contact with the Jino. The arrival of Hani, Yi and Han merchants to Jino Mountains is dated after 1729. Legends about the establishment of Yanuo village suggest that the Jino left Jiezhou Mt after a Han treacherous attack, which fits quite well with the historical data.

"Akha and Jinuo highlanders harvested tea leaves, which were sold to Chinese merchants who had begun to flock to this region, known as the "Six Great Tea Hills." Some of the finer teas... allegedly picked by girls trying to earn money for their bridal trousseaux, were sent as tribute to Beijing, and could be found in the houses of Beijing's elite" (Giersch 2006: 52).

The relationship between these Chinese merchants and the local populations, including the Jino, was not always as peaceful as desired, as "one local history claims that a Chinese merchant engaged in illicit sexual relations with a highlander woman." Being under the authority of the Xishuangbanna kings they complained not only about this incident, but claimed that "tea merchants and migrants practiced usury and exploitation... their frustration could no longer be contained as both highlanders and Tai felt tremendous anger toward Chinese migrants and the Qing government. In late May, a hill person stabbed to death a Chinese merchant, then rallied others. The mob went a killing spree, murdering at least fifteen Chinese in the vicinity of Simao" (Giersch 2006: 53).

During the Qing Dynasty Yongzheng emperor era Youle District was established at Situ, in the south of the Jino lands, in order to control them. This first attempt to control them was not very successful and was abandoned soon later. Still remains its ruins, with parts of a wall, a gate and a well. Jino legends still remember the hardships they suffered to build this city. Qing chronicles state that there was around 32 Jino (Youle) villages at this time (just 2 multiplied by 2 four times). A tumu or governor was appointed to rule these lands, which possibly resided in Bapu village and had only a limited power over the Jino. This also suggests that patriarchal tendencies and changes in indigenous leadership were related with the growing presence of Han people during the Qing dynasty (Zhang 2012: 8).

The integration of the Jino into the Chinese world was carried at by the Dai leaders, who were left in charge of apply locally the policies carried out by emperor Yongzheng. In some rituals the Dai nobles of Xishuangbanna made the chief of Situ village to act as his ancestor in these lands, calling him godfather. The king married a girl from Bapo, whose son became the 12th king of Xishuangbanna. Among the Jino the Dai have people responsible for collecting tributes and keeping the law in Jino lands. The structure of power created in the 1730s lasted until the 1930s (Zhang 2012:10).

Relationship with the Dai

The history of the Jino is closely linked to that of the Dai. In the past, the Dai Kingdom of Xishuangbanna extended north to present day Puer. Several ethnic groups, living as the Jino mainly in the mountains, had to pay to the Dai rulers different taxes (land tax, cotton tax) and provide free labor to comply their particular tasks (Wang).

Sometimes Dai local chiefs established alliances with the heads of the Jino clans or villages through marriage with Jino women, who became one of their many wives (Wang). Historical legends show that even the Dai King of Xishuangbanna took sometimes Jino wives. Dai historical records narrate that in 1390 the king took a Jino wife, a woman that played an important role in the politics of the time, and as mother of the next king, kept her influence until her death. This fact is preserved also in the Jino popular legends. This means that in these years the Jino people were already living in their present territory and that they had at least sporadic contacts with the Dai.

These notices of marriages between local princesses and foreign kings could be related to the Tibeto-Burman tradition of the transmission of political power through marriage with the daughters of the chiefs. Christine Mathieu (2003) described that historically the Naxi people transferred political power through the chief's daughters. That means that chiefs become chiefs only for their marriage with the daughter of the former chief. In *Matriarchy in China* (Ceinos 2011) we show that the founders of the two royal lineages of Nanzhao and Dali Kingdom ascended to power after marrying the daughters of powerful local lords. In can also be suggested that the unification of the six main polities (Six zhaos) under the leadership of Piluoge, the king of Nanzhao, only became effective when he performed, at least a ritual marriage, with the wives of the killed kings of the other zhaos. Marriages between Jino "princesses" and Dai local chiefs must have occurred at a time when most of the Jino villages were possibly governed by the oldest matriarch. These marriages would explain the secular friendship between the Jino and the Dai, and maybe were considered by the Dai rulers as a way to secure the dominion of Jino lands.

These links at the highest levels of political power had its correspondence at local level and even at individual level. At local level there was a kind of brotherhood between Jino and Dai leaders, cemented also in matrimonial alliances. At certain times the Dai chiefs would discuss local issues with their Jino counterparts: establishing or confirming territorial boundaries, banning the illegal cutting of trees, or solving interethnic conflicts such as buffalo destruction of crops. The general rule to establish the boundary line between Dai and Jino was: *the place with water pool for feeding buffalo was Dai's territory; and the place with wild banana trees was Jino's territory* (Wang).

At individual level friendship and cooperation was channeled through the *laogan* relations: a kind of brotherhood established between Jino and Dai individuals living in neighboring communities, to create exchange webs between two worlds very different at the eyes of their inhabitants, with many economic, social and political functions. Laogan relations were important "as a necessary product flow between upland and lowland for their livelihood" as well as a vehicle for "friendship sharing, information exchange and economic cooperation" (Wang).

Each Jino had some Dai laogan and vice versa. Once a boy or girl became ten years old their parents chose one or two appropriated aged Dai boys or girls as son's or daughter's *laogan* from their own network. They established these relationships in a hereditary basis, that is, as sons of laogan, or by personal choice. To emphasize the common fate of two laogan these links were usually established between two people born in the same year. To the Dai, a Jino laogan means the gate of the unknown world of the mountains, while to the Jino a Dai laogan was the gate of the world of contacts and relations in the lowlands.

Laogan relations show the complementarity of the Jino and Dai economies, and the need to establish a symbiotic relation between them. The Dai needed building materials, piglets (they did not grow mother pigs), banana leaves, and forest products used to season their food and make tools; the Jino however, demanded rice, tobacco, vegetables from the valleys, and cotton clothes. Although the economic interchanges were very important, laogan relations go beyond them, to include also political relations, sometimes facing a common enemy, informative, labor exchange, being the times of maximum activity different in valleys and mountains, and hospitality, as

41

laogan brothers were supposed to mutually provide accommodation if required, plus drinking water and food (Wang).

Rebellion of 1941

In 1930s the Government of the National Party in the Republic of China tried to reinforce their control over Jino lands to use all the resources of the small fragment of China that they controlled to fight against the Japanese invaders (Zhang 2012). The arrival of modern culture in Jino Mountains and the efforts of their religious leaders to adapt to a world that they started to perceive to be very different from their traditional reality, led to the creation in the 1930s of a syncretistic religion. Sang Yao, a religious leader of Baka village, is credited with this task. In the same way as other visionary prophets one night he woke up trembling with the feeling that a voice was telling him he must speak on behalf of the spirits of the Jino. He preached to the villagers that under the guidance of goddess Amoyaobai and the Chinese gods; the Jino must follow their own path. Among the deities of the new religion there was also Zhuge Liang, the Buddhist goddess of mercy Guanyin, the celestial master of Nine Ears, Guanshen Diqun, etc.

He ordered to close the gates of the spirits in all of the villages, which because they were used as protection against the evil spirits, were considered a symbol of the old religion. At the end of the uprising in many villages the gates of the spirits remained closed forever. Traditional ceremonies related to bailabao and mopei goddesses were discontinued; and many myths and rituals related to them were lost forever (Yu 2000: 104).

The government efforts to wipe out this religious movement provoked a Jino uprising in 1941 against the national government. Armed with their primitive weapons people from all the villages joined the fight. They resisted until April 1943, when they were definitively defeated. The short and discontinuous fighting that characterized this forgotten war brought great suffering to the Jino. In 1940 there were 6,000 Jino people in 42 villages, in 1951 they were only 3,600 living in 28 villages. The war, and the disasters linked with it, hunger, abandon of crops and tea garden, killing of big animals, epidemics, all took its toll on them (Yu 2000: 35).

Post – communist reforms

Following the establishment of the People's Republic in 1949, the reforms in Jino lands started in 1958. The socioeconomic foundations of the Jino culture were dismantled in favor of a central planning system that resulted in total dependency on the state. As their territory was a designated forest zone and their villages were dispersed amongst the the mountains, their culture still had a chance to be retained kept and still had time to adapt to the new economic and social conditions.

Standard agricultural techniques probed not suitable for Jino lands, and after the implementation of reforms, its production decreased. Government projects were met with considerable indifference by Jino communities. Because the living standards of some farmers in mountainous areas dropped after the implementation of the land reform, some of them preferred to go back to their slash and burn agriculture. The rehabilitation of old production methods proved effective (Bai and Zhang 2000: 34-5).

These new policies brought environmental changes to the Jino Mountain: The forest coverage decreased and biodiversity was destructed, the soil erosion and mountain landslide intensified. As a result the Jino had less arable land area and the cycle of crop rotation was reduced from the former average of 13 years to 7 and even 4 years in some places. The reduction of the rotation cycle aggravated soil erosion, which was especially dangerous as most of the slopes of Jino Mountain are between 20° and 50° (Zhao 1995: 15).

Economic reforms in Jino territory effectively started after the visit of President *Jiang Zemin* to their lands in 1989, when he exhorted: 'Our *Jino* brothers must be made prosperous as soon as possible.'' His words were the start of a new wave of changes that transformed once more the life of the Jino, with the monetary income of each person rising from an average of 800 yuan in the year 2000 to 1,614 yuan in 2004 (Guo 2007: 57).

Chapter 3

Religion of the Jino

The Jino concept of the spiritual world is based on three beliefs. The first is that the world is populated by a multitude of spirits continuously generated, which in some circumstances could be potentially harmful to human beings. The second is that people have a secure territory in the village situated behind the spirits gate, and the third is that in order to deal with the possible dangers of unknown spirits, human beings can rely on the help of a pantheon of goddesses and on the protection of the ancestors of their own family.

The Jino believe that each person has a body and soul. The material body performs the activities of a person's life under the guidance and protection of the spiritual soul. The protective role of the soul is especially important in the case of dangerous events. Not only do human beings have souls, but all living beings have one. In their minds, grasses, trees, birds and forest animals are all intelligent and moral, as are mountains, rivers and other natural phenomena. These spirits that animate each natural phenomenon can be found everywhere. They don't have a clear distinction between gods and devils, both are considered powerful spirits that can cause illness and disgraces when offended by human beings (Zhao 1995: 14).

Ancestral souls are also spirits, those belonging to other's family are feared as devils but those of their own family cannot be harmful and are therefore not feared (Cheng 1993). Mountain deities are the object of frequent ceremonies, as they are considered responsible of hunting and good harvest but also have the power to cause misfortune to men. They sacrifice before them piglets, chickens, and especially dogs, as the dog meat is rich in yang component, which can be beneficial to the growing of plants, essentially yin.

Men have nine souls and women, seven. Nine being the number usually related to males and seven to females, something they have in common with many peoples in south China and cultures around the world. Among the Jino these numbers are related to their primordial myth. After the flood Mahei and Maniu planted some gourds; while some of these gourds died, there were two that survived, and eventually one of them extended to nine rivers and mountains and blossomed into nine flowers, and the other extended to seven rivers and mountains, and gave origin to animals, plants, and human beings (Cheng 1993)

They have a dual view of the world in which life and death are two complementary aspects of each person's existence. They don't believe in paradise or hell. The place where they led the spirits of the dead, Sijiezhuomi is a world as real as the material world of the living people, where the dead follow similar lives. It is in fact the place that the ancestors of the Jino inhabited in the past. The realm of the living and that of the dead are the same world, being the village gate the boundary between their territories. These realms are separated by a river (Jile River) that only the dead can cross. This special arrangement responds to the idea that when humans and ancestors divided the world, humans accepted to take care of domestic animals and the spirits were kept in charge of the animals of the natural world. That means that when men go to hunt, they take animals from the spirits realm and must repay them with a sacrifice (Yu 2000: 98, 105). This idea was fully developed in Naxi religion, where the relationship between men and spirits of nature became the central point of their religious and ceremonial life (Ceinos: 2012).

They have many taboos regarding their use of land, animals and plants, which helped them to preserve an environment that they depend on to live. To the ancestral spirits and good spirits, they pray for a good harvest and good health for them and for their animals; to the evil spirits that can cause disasters to humans, they ask to be lenient (Grand 1999: 341).

Jino goddesses

Goddesses occupy the main positions in Jino mythology and religion, but they have no images or temples to focus their cult. All of their three main deities are goddesses: Amoyaobai the creator and the ancestral mother, Apierer the ancestor of human beings, and Peimo, the goddess of birth and fate (Cheng 1993). Among them, the most important is mother Amoyaobai, a giant of inexhaustible force worshipped each year in the Luomaluo Festival. The story of her creation of the world is their main myth, it tells that at the beginning of the times she arrived in this world and created all what exist. She separated heaven and earth, gave form to mountains, rivers and plains, and put on them plants, animals, and human beings. She established the equilibrium between human beings and animals and protected the human beings from the seven suns that threatened the world. She is the mother that created all what exists, a mother that protected her children and that assumed a central role in their old society.

47

From the flood there only survived a brother and sister floating inside a wooden drum. The new humanity surged from a gourd, whose seed was saved by the couple, which grew and grew until nurture inside it a new generation of human beings. The ancestral couple knew that inside the gourd a new humankind wanted to come out, but each time they tried to burn the gourd to open a hole, they listened to a voice that said: "No. Don't burn here, I am here." At the end the ancestral mother Apierer asked them to burn just where she stood. They burnt her navel. She died but the human beings came out of the gourd. The Jino believe they are the offspring of this goddess, and they keep a special respect for her as she sacrificed herself for human beings.

Peimo is the goddess of birth and fate. Her spirit enters the fetus when he is two months old, and draws some wrinkles in his forehead and his hands, that will define his future fate. When a woman cannot get pregnant, the bailapao priest performs a ceremony to Peimo, asking her to give a child (Grand: 341). She stores the unborn children in the mythic land known as Tailuomenmo, where the three main goddesses have their own villages, from where she will send them to the earth on the moment of conception. This Tailuomenmo or Kingdom of Goddesses is also the place where the bailabao, mopei and blacksmith go after death, to reunite with the goddesses which with they are spiritually married, and the place from which they get their magic skills in their ceremonies. A Kingdom of Goddesses from where all the life and power originate (Outlook 1999).

Sacred to all the Jino are the three goddesses of the shellfish. Nufayishou is the shellfish Goddess of Thunder or of Heaven. She is also the goddess of fate. Some people think that she is a transformation of Peimo. She can transform herself into a shellfish and go down to the humans' world, where she will marry a man who would become a bailapao, in charge of the religious rituals and sacrificial activities. Fugaomishe is the shellfish goddess of grain. She is in charge of all the agricultural and production process. She also can turn herself into a shellfish and descend to the earth to pair with a man. She is known also as Qiaomuasheng[1], she is able to provide the people with a good harvest, and cares about the proper growth of rice, so the main ceremonies related to the agricultural cycle are performed to her (Eorc. 547-8). Lateyishuo, the shellfish goddess of the mountain, is in charge of hunting and gathering activities. These deities are represented as shells, symbols of the female sex. The bailapao shamans have the ability to travel between this world and the dead world; praying for people and curing their illnesses, are considered to speak on behalf of them. The goddess of the Jino shamans (mopei in their language) is Peimo, and that of the ironsmith is Mentaimizhi. Ironsmith, priest and shamans perform activities that put in communication the people and the spirits of illnesses. Bailabao and Beimo goddesses work together, the former care about divination, the later about the way the result will be used to heal a sick person.

Among the Aha and Axi branches, shells are attributed only to the bailapao; among the Wuyou branch, are symbols of spiritual beings. Children usually wear them in their hats, with three pieces of ginger, and when one a person die, he must carry a shellfish to cross the border between the world of the living people and the world of shadows and join the ancestors' realm. Among the Jino shells, the first currency in the Chinese

---

[1] Goddesses and spirits in general have usually different names in different Jino villages.

world, seem to play the same role that coins play in other funerary traditions.

Below these main goddesses there is a legion of minor goddesses governing almost every natural phenomena and geographic accident, sometimes called by different names in different places. They have goddesses of fire (Mishengmikao), of water (Choushentuomi), of earth, of mountains, of the forest, and of different game (Cheng 1993: 25). Leisi is the Goddess of the bamboo forest. According to their legends there were two young lovers that, belonging to the same clan and knowing that they cannot marry, flew to the forest. There she lived in the upper part of the forest and he in the lower part, meeting occasionally in the middle. When the sister died the brother felt so sad that he frequently went to the middle part of the forest to long for her; where he received some gifts. Later the hunters imitated him making offerings to this goddess in the middle part of the mountain forest to ask her to give them some of her animals (Grand). Xiaosi is the deity in charge of the big hunt: deer, wild boar, bear, wild ox, goat, etc. When a hunter hunts one of these animals, he must perform a ceremony in that spot. At home he must perform a new ceremony to this deity that must be led by the zhuoba if he hunted a wild ox. Shexi is the Deity of rodents. When the hunter gets a small rodent he must perform a small ceremony to her. Esi is the deity of the birds. Called Api in other places. The more than 70 species of birds that the Jino regularly hunt are governed by her (Grand 342, Eorc 508). Goddesses of the Cross Roads are the deities that control the crossing of nine roads where the souls of the dead must pass, and only let pass the good souls. Blacksmith, bailapao and mopei, after death, need their respective goddesses to pass those cross roads (Eorc-87).

Rain is created by the Mother of Rain. Thunder is attributed to their ancestral mother, the Mother of Thunder (Chatou in some villages) who according to their legends is always grinding. If her pounding stone is turned upside up in heaven there is thunder and human beings on earth can be hit by lightning. To avoid it, on the sixth month they sacrifice a pig and some chickens to her (Eorc 795; Du 1996). They think that if a house, tree, animal or person is hit by thunder it is a punishment or an omen from this deity. This place became the abode of demons and people avoid it. Then they hold a ceremony offering a pig and a chicken on a bamboo pole with some thunder designs, smearing the animal's blood and a *dailuo* for protection. (Grand: 342). Dishen, the deity of the earth, is in charge of the nine columns that sustain the earth. When there is an earthquake they pray to him to stop moving the earth. Muli is the deity of the mountain, in charge of animals and vegetables living on it. They worship the spirit of stone in some places, as well as the spirit of the ant hill, the spirit of fire, and the spirit of epidemics. They never destroy the den of hedgehogs and even try to protect them, thinking that they are the abode of powerful spirits. Big trees also have powerful spirits.

In some villages the village deity is called Zhuomi Shangba. She is considered the deity of the zhuoba. The three ceremonies performed every year in her honor must be lead by the zhuoba, who will pray for the wellbeing and prosperity of all the members of the village. A Liu spirit inhabits the spirit room of each long-house. Offerings are presented to this deity after a good hunt and a solemn ceremony is performed on the 4th month. The spirits of the parents of the long-house are often worshipped, as they are considered the representatives of the ancestor that established the long house. When a new head of the family or zhaole is chosen all the family must worship the family deity (Zheng 2008: 100-2).

Decai is the goddess of the blacksmith (Mentaimizhi in other accounts). Due to the importance of iron in the Jino culture she is highly veneered. To become a blacksmith a person must go through a complex process. It starts when something strange happens, such as dreaming that he will be a blacksmith, or find animals in pairs when he goes hunting, signs that the goddess is choosing him to be a blacksmith. Then the bailapao must divine if he has been really chosen by the goddess. Later there will be a ceremony in which he will arrange the blacksmith instruments and become one. He has ritual importance in the village, as his dreams are interpreted before Temaoke festival (Grand: 341).

In this world full of spiritual beings humans encounter with goddesses are not feared but actively sought, as they are considered to appear before the people as girls with flowers. It usually happens when a goddess sees a man she likes and she wants to marry him. These marriages can last from the short time spiritual pairings between hunters and the Goddess of Hunt to the all the life compromises between shamans and the goddesses that guarantee their powers to deal with unknown and sometimes dangerous spirits. If a hunter manages to hunt any animal it is because the goddess of hunt gives it to him; so, to be a good hunter it is important that the hunter establishes a relationship with the goddess. If a man hunts a deer, the hunter would sleep three nights with Xiaosi goddess, who is in charge of the deer, as if he was married to her for three days. If somebody acts as bailapao or mopei it is because the respective goddess is inside him, because he married her. One man can marry once with a human woman, but many times with goddesses (Cheng 1993).

The Jino relationship with the Goddess of the Grain, Zhaogaomizhe, essential for their feeding and survival, is managed by women, although they think that this goddess also can go down to earth to pair with a mortal man. Each year during the third month, before sowing seeds, they hold a ceremony to call upon this goddess. Days later the women of each household go to the fields to sow, and the most important woman of each family, ritually dressed, goes to the fields to pray and worship her (Eorc 97).

Amainei are spirits of the trees, vines, rocks or water that can produce illness or misfortune to human beings. Chu are water deities that can cause illness to people. They inhabit the pools and ponds. When somebody is sick and the bailapao divines that the sickness was caused by a Chu, they would lay a dog half buried with the mouth towards the pool as sacrifice to him. Then they will put around the dog taro and daliu and other objects that can keep evil spirits away. The spirits of the big trees are very dangerous and can harm people, so they pray to them during some ceremonies. The spirits of some vines are the transformations of devils that can eat people and make them feel sick. Teqie is a deity that after his death his leg became a green tree, his hand a vine and other parts of his body different natural objects. When a person member's aches they think it is because he hit a tree, a vine or other part of this deity. Zhuopu is the deity of the ant-houses, he is worshipped when children get sick, when they take a bowl used by him before the ant-house to pray for a quick recovery (Grand: 341).

The Jino believe in the existence of a kind of devils who eat human beings called teche. These teche live in the villages, like the common people, and are supposed to make the people disappear in mysterious ways and cause harm to recently buried corpses. They believe these devils are afraid of a wooden tablet called Techeayue, used by the Jino to counteract their influences. Though they think there are not teches anymore, when they bury their dead they stick bamboo, wood or stone knives, to keep the teches off (Eorc 677).

Religious specialists

Their main religious specialists are bailabao, mopei and zhalai or Blacksmith. The oldest man of the main clan in the village is called zhuoba or mother of the village; the oldest of the second clan is the zhuosheng or father of the village. They have as leader of the village, important ritual functions, presiding over the most important ceremonies and rituals. The oldest woman in the village, called youka, also has some ritual functions. It is possible that in the past most of the clan leaders were women and maybe shamans: the wisest shamans that could divine omens and chant incantations, as they are credited with the first improvements in human civilization.

It seems that the power held nowadays by the religious specialists is a heritage of that of the legendary shamanesses, and, as the spiritual power belongs to women, they must feminize themselves. Sometimes when male shamans conduct rituals, they are required to dress as women, or they need to get married symbolically to a goddess.

While the zhuoba and zhuosheng are ritual leaders, bailapao and mopei are associated with shamans. Both bailapao and mopei were hereditary posts (Cheng 1993). Ironsmiths, priests and shamans, due to their dependence on the goddesses, must ritually marry a goddess. From the moment when the love for the goddess is manifested to the time when the ritual wedding is celebrated there are certain steps.

54

The start is a casual encounter with the goddess who is looking for a representative on earth; usually a strange thing happens that only can be explained for as divine intervention, such as appearing and disappearing of shellfish, which is considered a sign that the goddess of the shellfish is playing with him. Then they ask an old bailapao to divine if the person that suffered this experience has really been before the goddess. To do it he must perform a ceremony for the goddess of shellfish with offerings of pigs and other animals, and must even sacrifice a cow. Before the sacrifice of a cow a very important ceremony is performed, when the old bailapao, before an improvised altar, produces two shellfish enacting the ritual marriage between the new bailapao and the goddess of the shellfish. If the result is positive they must inform the chief of the village, who would advise him about a ritual marriage, in which he would act as witness. Then they must build a house for the bride goddess in the groom's home, which a size of 30 cm high. Inside it they put a nuptial bed. Then they chose an auspicious date and celebrate the proper wedding, sacrificing a cow. Under the sound of drums and cymbals, the old shaman helps the groom to go near the goddess, doing some magic tricks to make her presence known to everybody. At the end they invite the goddess to go live in the new house, and from then on they consider that this man has two wives: the goddess and his mortal wife.

After this ceremony the old bailapao would instruct the new one during some time until the moment when he can perform ceremonies by himself. Later he will build his own altar to the shellfish goddess, consisting of a wood panel with many shellfish hanging from it, and he would place his divination objects below the altar, and make his ritual dress black color and a ritual cap of the same color, decorated with strips of many colors and with many shellfish hanging. His ritual implements include two ritual swords, a female one used inside the house, and a male one to be used outside, a pole and a paper fan, that are usually kept on the altar (Cheng 1993).

Bailabao usually has some knowledge of medicinal plants. There are two kinds of bailapao, some are the common ones that cannot carry on the most important rituals, but perform divination and healing, and the big bailapao, that can carry on the most important ceremonies (Du 1996). Their main task is to divine for the ill. One of the ways of divining consist that the family of the ill person brings the bailapao a cloth of the sick with a piece of ginger, a bunch of salt and an egg inside. The bailapao must put these things on his altar and put a shellfish on a teacup or the nail of his thumb finger. Then he will recite three times the name of the spirits that could have caused the sickness, and when he says the name of the incumbent spirit, he would feel, thanks to the shellfish, that this is the one responsible for the sickness. Then the family would ask a mopei to expel this spirit. Sometimes they divine putting rice grains with some shellfish inside a bowl or a teacup and would proceed to whisper the names of the evil spirits. When he whispers one name he would take a handful of rice and shellfish from the cup, and if both rice and shellfish are in even numbers, it is considered that the spirit named is the responsible (Cheng 1993). Other divination methods include examining the thigh bone of a chicken. To do it they first sacrifice the chicken, cook it, and take out the thigh bone. They clean it and insert two fine bamboo sticks. If the bamboo sticks remain in a vertical position it is auspicious, if not, problems can happen. They also divine by boiling the claws of the chicken and of other animals, examining its tongue and its head, etc. (Du 1996).

If a cow or a pig must be sacrificed, is also the task of the bailapao, who has a higher ritual status. When a bailapao goes to another village he usually has a helper to open his way, and most of the members of his family and of the family of the sick person, following him. He will be rewarded by his work with money and part of the offerings presented in the ceremony (Cheng 1993).

The mopei is in charge of expelling evil spirits. A common person can become a mopei when he is chosen by Peimo goddess. After experiencing strange things he is considered to be the aim of the goddess Peimo and an old mopei performs a ceremony to link them. Later, he will make a bamboo altar that will hang from one of the posts of his house's door. Below it he will set a small table with some offerings. He is ritually dressed with a black hat with feathers, a black coat and a ritual stick to beat the earth during his ceremonies. Bailapao and mopei usually work together. Bailapao divines, but he can't subdue evil spirits; the magic powers of the mopei are higher. He can directly contact the evil spirits and subdue them. As the Jino think that evil spirits are everywhere, the mopei is called not only in case of sickness, but when they erect a new house, celebrate a marriage or a funeral.

In the wedding ceremony the mopei must take the spirit of the bride from her parents' house to the groom's house. (It must be noted that among the Naxi, the main ritual in the wedding is to take the bride spirit to the groom's house). In the funerals he must chant prayers to avoid the deceased soul linger near his former house that could cause problems to his descendants. To raise a new house he must pray to heaven for the safety of the house, and to choose the proper trees to make its main posts. He has also a relevant role in the ceremonies that involved the whole village, such as the ceremony for the

Village Deity, when he accompanies the zhuoba praying for the wellbeing and the prosperity of the village and the prayers to the Deity of Thunder when there is a draught. He is also the healer that must perform ceremonies of ghost expelling and soul searching (Cheng 1993, Yu 2000: 102).

Jino blacksmith are called zhalai, they are ritually the second most important person in each village. To be an ironsmith the bailapao must divine that the goddess Dailuomengmo is approaching this person. Then he holds a ceremony for this goddess, and he will arrange a set of instruments to be offered in his home (Outlook 1999). During New Year ceremonies the blacksmith is always beside the zhuoba, he can offer wine to the wooden drum and has the privilege of not taking off his hat before the drum (while other villagers, including the zhuoba, must do) (Eorc: 822). The ability of the blacksmith to smelt iron is considered to be granted to him by the Goddess of the Blacksmith. Blacksmiths importance in Jino society is not only due to their ability to make the tools needed for hunting and agricultural activities, but also for their ritual role in village ceremonies, especially in the Jino New Year or Temaoke, when the main blacksmith must sacrifice before his goddess asking her to provide himself with good dreams. Next morning he will play the main role in a tell-the-dreams ceremony, when omens regarding the coming year are supposed to be conveyed by the Goddess. Some iron foundry ceremonies require killing a chicken and pouring its blood and feathers on the fire, asking the fire deities to protect the fire and allow a good smelting process.

These ceremonies show that although their society changed from matriarchy to patriarchy, men cannot occupy the role that traditionally occupied women without their help. A similar relationship is established between the hunter and Xiaosi the

Goddess of Hunt, which according to their legends was a woman who died for love. If the goddess is happy they think game will be good, so when the hunter gets good game he must stay three days without sleeping with his wife, so as to not offend the goddess. Religious leaders only need to wait until the moment of their death to join the goddesses in the place they inhabit and enjoy a common life with them (Yu 2000: 102).

Although ritual marriages between men and goddesses were not so developed in Chinese culture, the spiritual marriage between Taoist practitioners and the Queen Mother of the West (Xiwangmu) was considered during the Tang dynasty as a suitable gate to reach immortality. Though this process, as depicted in Susanne Cahill's (1993) book, it seems to be focused more on the individual pursue of immortality than in the public services important to the Jino shamans, this could suggest that with the strain of cultural influences which changed the respective roles of men and women in Jino society, some Taoist ideas could have arrived to Jino lands and contributed to the establishment of a new paradigm of relationship with the spirits world in which men displaced women of their former post and carried out ritual marriage with these divinized women that were their goddesses.

Neique are people that can release the spirits. It is supposed that they can put spirits in a place and harm other people, making them fall sick or even die. They are feared and hated by the people, and are usually forced to keep lonely lives or can even be killed by other people if they think they are responsible for their disgraces. Shichao are spirits that have the shape of a person and can talk, but they eat people. They can become leopards or wild cats and eat the heart of the children and pregnant women. At first they can hunt with people, but later

59

they eat all the game, or, if there is no game, eat the hunter. Later the Jino discovered their nature and sought ways of avoiding them (Cheng 1993: 35; Grand: 341). Geqi are considered half doctors half shamans. They have no special role in religious ceremonies but they can divine and know the cause of sickness. Their special powers are usually hereditary. When they die they cannot be buried, but must be cremated (Dict: 330).

Rituals

Along the history the Jino have devised a set of ceremonies usually performed to appease the spirits. The most important of them are:

Ceremony to expel the spirit of fire. It is performed when fires happens frequently. They put a burnt wooden log in a sedan, and then smear it with the blood of a pig that has been sacrificed to the fire spirit. Later they carry the sedan out of the village shouting the fire spirit to leave. When a fire occurs in a village, village people cannot go to another village, for fear that they carry with them the spirit of fire (Cheng 1993).

Aheluoka is a ceremony performed when the village faces a disaster: epidemic illness, many deaths, sickness of their animals, repeated fires, because they consider that all these misfortunes are caused by evil spirits, all the men pray to the deity of the village, with wooden swords and guns, and offer him a pig and some chickens. They made some animal figurines with clay, which they offer to their god. Later, inside each house, male members perform a magic dance with their wooden swords to expel the evil spirits. At the end, they made a sedan and put inside clay figurines of persons and animals, and take it outside the village under the sound of firecrackers, symbolizing that they carry away the evil spirits (Cheng 1993, Dict: 329). It is important to remember that in Naxi rituals used to expel evil spirits which cause sickness, these evil spirits are ritually transferred to clay figurines, called *duoma* among them, and then discarded (Ceinos 2012).

Ceremony to call the soul. They think that the people get sick because their soul leaves them, usually after being scared. So the soul must be called back. To do it first a bailapao must divine to know where the soul is. He carries a basket with a chicken or a hen (depending on the sex of the ill person), some silver wares, etc., and at the supposed place where the soul is hidden, he will call him in a loud voice asking for him to call back home (Cheng 1993). If a child gets sick the mother makes a simple ceremony, offering a chicken to her deceased parents and asking them to heal the child; if the sickness become serious they ask the mopei to divine the whereabouts of the soul, then the mother will go to this place with some clothes and offerings to call the soul of the child. She will ask the soul to not remain there but come back to its dwelling (Du 1996).

These ceremonies seem related to rituals performed in China thousands of years ago, as de Groot writes: "When a baby is taken with convulsions, the affrighted mother finding her first attempts to coax her darling back to consciousness by repeatedly calling out its name to be in vain, she hastens up to the roof of her house and, waving about a bamboo pole to which is affixed a garment belonging to the little one, exclaims several times in succession: «My child so-and-so, come back, return home!» In the interim another inmate of the house loudly beats a gong, to arouse the attention of the soul... the custom of calling back the dead was highly developed in China in olden times... a suit of the deceased was made to play an important part in the ceremony. "They used the clothes he was want to wear during his lifetime, supposing that the vital spirits, on recognizing them, would re-enter them and seek refuge therein" (Groot, I : 243).

Sometimes sick people are treated also with herbal medicines, and animal sacrifices are offered to the spirits. Most of the oxen, pigs, chicken and dogs raised by the Jino, are used for sacrifices to get rid of demons. A good way of strengthening the body when it is weakened (Zhi 1984).

Sending off the spirit of epidemics is performed on a regular basis three times a year to avoid epidemic diseases. Worshiping the pond is performed if draught happens, when zhuoba sacrifices three pigs (Cheng 1993: 23).

Sacred paraphernalia

Wood drums are the most sacred object of the Jino; they are a symbol of the village. In fact in each Jino village there is a pair of drums; a mother drum which is hung in the zhuoba's house, and a father drum which is hung in the zhuosheng's house. They are considered the embodiment of the divine spirits and therefore cannot be handled except during sacred ceremonies or festivals, when they are prayed upon to provide well being, a bountiful harvest, and prosperity to the people, and to ward off disease off the people and animals. Then the drum is taken out for the drum dance, the most representative dance of the Jino. Among the Wa nationality wooden drums have similar consideration.

The making of a drum is full of taboos, as well as the change of its skin-hide, when the drum is placed in a hut outside the village and its spirit is prayed to every day so not give up on this place while the hide is changed. In the prayers they call the drum "father and mother of the clan", "father of the village", "mother of the village". Because there are two drums in the village, one in the house of each of the clan leaders, it seems that in the past the drum was the protector of the clan, and not of the village. Identification of the drum with the clan is also common among Yao communities living in Guangxi Province. When a zhuoba or zhuosheng dies the people stop working for a day. The drum is placed in a slant, and a ceremony is held to carry it to the new zhuoba's house. He must receive the drum with new clothes and flowers, and a ceremony is performed in which he will offer three chickens, one to his parents, one to the village god and one to the spirit of the drum (Cheng 1993: 32).

The drum is considered sacred because in mythical times it saved the ancestral brother and sister, Maniu and Mahei, from the flooding. The drum is also a symbol of the sun worshipped by the Jino. It has an array of 17 wooden tubes symbolizing rays of light. They consider the sun-drum a reincarnation of a god and a symbol of the village, believing that it can bless all the people living there.

Daliu, a net made of bamboo strips of different sizes, and ginger are considered the main protectors used to keep away evil spirits. There is a history that narrates the origin of the use of these two magical talismans. At first when people died, they become spirits which the living people fed, but with the passing of time, spirits were more and more numerous and the living people had difficulties in feeding so many spirits. There was an old couple whose only son died. They feed his spirit for some time, but later it was impossible for them to feed him. As he only ate and slept, they tried to make him work, but he complained that because he was a spirit he couldn't work. His parents tried several methods to keep him away, at least one day they gave him ginger to eat, asking him to not come back until he finished eating the ginger. But the ginger was so spicy that he had no way to eat it. When he came back home asking for more food, his mother said that if he did not eat all the ginger she would not give him any more food. Then he went to his father, who was weaving a bamboo basket into the shape of a daliu. He told the spirit of his son that if he knew exactly how many holes there were in the daliu, he will feed him. But the son failed and the parents were able to get rid of him. Later, many people learn about it and they also used ginger and daliu to keep the spirits away (Cheng 1993: 37). Taro can also keep away evil spirits. It is buried when a new house is erected and also when somebody is sick. Chicken and dog blood also have the same power, as well as metal objects.

Chapter 4

The Jino Life Cycle

Birth

The Jino believe that sons and daughters are given by Peimo the Goddess of Birth. Life is created by her, with women acting as her envoys. She brings the human soul stored in the mythical Kingdom of the Goddess to the fetus on the third month of pregnancy, and she provides the seven souls required for a woman or the nine for a man. She is also the goddess of fate, because human fate is determined at birth. As Jino believe their fate is carved in one's face and one's hands, from whence diviners can divine, they ask the Peimo goddess to provide new babies with auspicious wrinkles in both places (Yu 2000: 89).

They believe the gestation period for a female fetus is seven months, and nine months for a male one. When a woman is pregnant there are many taboos that the husband and wife must be sure to avoid. When the husband goes hunting he cannot beat monkeys, or the baby would not be beautiful, and he must avoid several birds with beautiful feathers or ugly singing to avoid other problems with the future child. He cannot engage in the public village ceremonies, nor take fruits from the trees or beat snakes, as the taken fruits put his own fruit in danger and the snake is a feminine symbol. The life of the pregnant mother also exhibits many changes. She is expected to pay increased attention to matters of everyday life. She must wear loose clothing, reduce her time in the fields and carry out fewer household chores. Pregnant women cannot eat banana flowers, because it is said that they can induce miscarriage. They eat fresh vegetables and meat instead of sour, cold, smelly or raw foods. They don't eat fruits that have been bitten by worms in fear that the baby may be born handicapped. They eat pheasants with colorful feathers and the meek bamboo rat in order to have a beautiful baby. They never say words such as "dumb", "deaf", "blind" or "dead" for fear of their baby's safety and future health (Zhao 1995 19-20).

Delivery must be carried out in the back terrace of their houses, usually in a kneeling position, which allows the mother to focus all her strength on the delivery process. With her family members around her, women experience less fear and anxiety. After birth, the umbilical cord is cut with bamboo scissors, and the placenta is placed inside a gourd and buried under the house facing the mother's bed. Later it is covered with a bamboo basket and surrounded by nine or seven sticks depending on the sex of the newborn, as each stick represents one of the souls of the baby. That night, a chicken must be killed and offered to the ancestors asking them to protect the newborn (Zhao 1995: 27).

At the moment of birth, the person beside the baby must immediately give him a name, in fear that without a name the spirits could take him away. They also hang on his or her neck nine or seven white threads to keep away evil spirits. Then the parents, in the goddess post (one of the main posts of the house), announce this birth to Peimo goddess and ask her to protect the newborn, avoiding sicknesses and bad spirits, and allowing him to grow up happily. Later they put some tree branches on the gate of their home to let the neighbors know that a baby is born and that nobody may enter the house, and they hang some leaves of the tung tree and bamboo in the gate to keep bad spirits away.

The first food for the mother must consist of the most beautiful birds and rodents, and if possible birds with beautiful songs. These are sometimes stored at home during pregnancy time, in order to guarantee that the newborn will be beautiful, as they believe that these animals can transmit their beauty and good qualities to the baby. Especially appreciated is squirrel soup, sometimes made with a freshly caught squirrel, thought to strengthen the newborn. After delivery, Jino women can eat neither chicken, pork nor big animals, but instead only vegetables and the meat of small animals (Cheng 1993: 54).

The following day, the father takes the spirit of the newborn to his hunt, as a way to ensure that in the future he will be a good hunter. Nine days after a child is born they celebrate the rite of calming the spirit, when the parents must kill two red-feathered chickens and a name is given by the sorcerer in charge of the rite (Song 2007: 306). On the thirteen day, the husband offers a chicken to the Goddess of the Hunt. During the first month he sleeps near the mother taking care of her. If the baby cries frequently they change his name (Cheng 1993: 40).

Before the first month of life the newborn is not considered to have the complete possession of a soul, and is not considered to be a full human being, as his spirit is yet one soul "drifting among the living world" (Zhao 1995: 11). To avoid possible dangers that could threaten mother and baby, during this time they must sleep in a special place, where outside visits are avoided. A *daliu* is hung on the stairs of the house to avoid evil spirits and the newborn is dressed in white, a symbol of light and cleanliness, as opposed to the darkness of the spirit world.

After this month the newborn is ritually carried out of the gate of the village and his clothes are changed to the same as the other children.

When the time comes to give a name to the child, Jino people follow the naming system common in other minorities where Yi-related languages are spoken, that is the consecutive naming system between father and children in which the last part of the name of the father is the first part of children's names. This common naming system is not followed in special circumstances. When the child has an incurable disease, then the connection can be broken, and the parents will choose another name for him, usually consecutive with that of a shaman or his title bailabpao, for it is said that the shaman's name could frighten the devils. When the child's brother or sister has died young before the child's birth, the parents worry that the newborn will follow this fate, and choose to break the connection. In this case, they use "Po" before the child's name, as the hard sound "po" can protect the child. When a woman is giving birth and the umbilical cord hangs around the child's neck or shoulders, which is considered a monstrous phenomenon, the connection should be broken and the child's name should start with "Sha". If the child is born on the road, his name will not be linked to his father's name but use "road" ("ya" in their language) instead. If someone from another village breaks the taboo and walks into the delivery room when the child is born, the child should acknowledge him as nominal father and repeat his name, to be protected by him to grow up healthily (Yunnan).

Rites of passage.

Age ceremonies are very important for the Jino; they mark moment when the individual becomes part of the society.

Before the age of fifteen Jino youngsters are not considered adults; they cannot have the responsibilities or the rights of adults, including the lack of freedom to leave their home at night and to talk about love. Their working time is counted and valued as half of that of the adults.

At the age of fifteen or sixteen, every teenager has his or her rite of passage called *wurere*, which marks the beginning of his or her adulthood, before the family and the whole village. This ceremony is performed sometimes at the same time as the rising of a new building or during the Temaoke festival. Usually people just snatch the young man suddenly without his knowledge and bring him to a gathering in the *raokao*, or youngster's club. The following day his parents give him a set of agricultural tools, clothes and other symbols of adulthood. During the ceremony the elders of the village sing traditional songs and poems to teach him the traditional culture and customs, moral norms and regulations, the productive cycle and of social life, as well as other aspects of their traditional education. Later the elders give him two small packets of meat from the sacrifices. Sometimes it includes a career-choosing ceremony where young men choose a trade (they ask experienced village craftsmen if they may serve as apprentices under them), and they are given the tools that they will need to do the trade they have chosen.

The ceremonies for women are less formal. The women are not usually captured, but instead secretly prepare an apron, wear it and appear in front of others in the streets or fields. From that point on, the girl wears her apron as an adult, and is accepted in the *mikao* youngster association. They also receive agricultural tools, new clothes and kitchen utensils, and change their hair style to that of an adult. When the ritual ends, all the people of the village sacrifice a cow and welcome them to the adult world (Cheng 1993: 44; Zhao 1995: 17).

After these ceremonies youngsters start to dress and behave as adults. Most importantly, they have the right to love and to be loved, and to participate in all public activities (Bai and Zhang 2000: 33). Their adulthood is emphasized by some bodily transformations. "Earlobes were pierced, teeth blackened, and tattoos applied to their bodies. Girls usually had only their legs tattooed, with lace-like patterns, while boys had their legs and shoulders decorated with designs of animals, flowers, grass, stars, and tools. The traditional belief was that people without tattoos do not join their ancestors after death and instead became wild ghosts" (Ye 1993: 151).

After the adulthood ceremony the young Jino spend the night out of their home, as they are enlisted in a youth organization called *raokao*, usually led by one of the older, cleverer or better singing youngsters. Integrated within this organization the young men start to participate in some community tasks, such as patrolling in festivals and religious ceremonies, and they become familiar with the productive ways, social norms, moral values and religious beliefs of their society. Some of them can join the *polei* society, where controls are stricter, and they must carefully follow Jino customary laws, as they will be in charge of punishing those who violate these laws. Young women on their side have the *mikao* organization, which also helps them to slowly become familiar with their new adult lives (Du 1991: 410-11).

Nigaozhou or "playing house" is the big house open to everybody, and where the young people gather in the evening. Sometimes it is a new building, or the house of some older fellows. Here, the young sing romantic songs, play music, make

70

jokes and talk about love. They usually spend the night there. But it is not a place to make love (Zheng 2008: 74). People in the *raokao* group protect laws and especially love traditions in the village. That is, they ensure that none of the youngster show unacceptable behavior. Though there is some variation between Jino villages, in some places when the boy leaves the *nigaozhou* to spend the night with his lover there is a small ceremony performed that marks the end of the coming of age, when a dog is sacrificed and a feast is offered to the whole village (Du 2008: 133).

Love and marriage

The special characteristics of Jino marriage are: that marriage takes place inside the village, but outside the clan. Only rarely do Jino people marry with people from another village or from another nationality. A couple live together before they are married. It suffices that the girl agrees to start living with her boyfriend. In some villages this step is prior to the marriage, while in others it is a more informal relation that can be broken at will, in a way that young people can have many lovers before they choose to marry one. The girl spends the night with her boyfriend, who must leave the house at dawn. It is common that children are born during this period. These children belong to the mother's side, but they will be "bought" by the husband's side at the time of marriage. Divorce is common and easy and can be started by either side. The process that leads to the marriage has five steps: adulthood, love, living together, choosing a wedding day, and the wedding ceremony (Zheng 2008: 178).

Only after being considered adults can young Jino fall in love and marry. They enjoy sexual freedom before marriage. Before 1949 it was common for 16 and 17-years-old to engage in premarital sex. Villages even had a special house for them to spend the night where they sing, play music, tell jokes or talk about love. Once a couple felt an attachment, the man would go quietly to his lover's family home late at night and sleep with her at night, but they must separate at dawn, when he must go back to his own house. During their nightly visits the girl arranges soot of pearl wood and asks her lover to dye her tooth. A child born of such union was not looked down upon, and the woman would take the child with her at the time of her wedding (Zhong 1983: 29; Zhang and Zeng 1993). Though spending the night together put a couple on the way to marriage, they can separate if they want and choose a new lover. These years relationships seem to be more like the walking marriage famous among the Moso with a complete freedom to choose their lovers. The main difference is that here, after the period of free love, the young couple is supposed to (but will not necessarily) marry and the woman will become part of a family directed by the husband. Before the marriage, the pairing was not mutually exclusive and had traces of the communal pairings of the past. Children born before marriage (about one third of Jino children) are supposed to belong to the mother's side. The husband must "buy" them with some gifts presented to her uncle during the wedding (Zheng 2008: 83).

When it comes to dating, it is usually the young woman who will first approach the young man. She makes him know that she likes him, sometimes she lightly steps on her lover's foot, gives him a tobacco-box, or touches his body invitingly (Du 1991: 412). The most special way to express their feelings is by means of flowers and tree leaves arranged in different ways. If a woman finds a young man attractive, she will pick the flower she likes best and give it to him and he will accept the flowers if he also likes her (Zhao 1995: 9). They bundle tree leaves in different ways and put them in the place they agreed on, as a present to their beloved. Different tree leaves, the distinct ways they are bundled and the place they are arranged are considered by each party to decipher the meaning which is wished to be conveyed. Sometimes leaves of more than one tree are combined, or are bundled with the hairs of the sender (Cheng 1993: 49).

After the couple has been together for between six months to three years they start to think of marrying; a business usually arranged by their parents. The family of the boyfriend goes to visit the girlfriend's family carrying wine and some small gifts. They discuss the feelings of the lovers and when they reach an accord, they drink together. In a second visit they discuss the details of the wedding and in a third one the date of the wedding is chosen (Du 1991: 413). In some Jino villages after the proposal of marriage to the bride's parents, "the young man must first go to live in the young woman's home for one to three years of "trial" marriage. The young man works hard from day to night in order to convince his lover's parents to allow the couple to formally marry as early as possible. Occasionally the young woman may go to help out at the young man's home" (Ye: 1993: 152). It cannot be doubted that this "trial marriage" is a remnant of past matrilocality, when after marriage the husband moved to live in his wife's home.

They do not have public engagement ceremonies but instead a private exchange of symbolic gifts. The groom usually presents his lover with a pair of brass bracelets, and she gives him a string made of dried red beans. These gifts symbolize unbreakable love and harmony. Some women put a betel nut directly into their lover's mouth as a sign that she is willing to be his wife. If a man cannot get any betel nut from the woman he loves he eventually gives up and searches for another lover.

"Betel nuts are used because their taste changes from bitter to sweet when chewed, meaning that the suitor must undergo a similar order of experience in the courtship" (Ye 1993: 151).

Though monogamous marriage is now the norm among them, remnants of previous marriage forms can be found in some of their traditions. Children born out of wedlock either go with the mother when she formally marries or stay with the maternal uncle. Marriages between brothers and sisters were common in the past, and today cousins are allowed to marry in some villages (Zhi 1984: 150). They address their relations according to generations, not sex. Grandson and granddaughters are all called *lirao*; sons and daughters, nephews and nieces all are called *raozuo*. Gender-free terms of address reflect that in the past people of the same generation could marry each other (Song 2007). In their society there is no ill treatment or abandonment of children, nor any preference regarding for the gender of their children. Sons and daughters are desired equally. To have daughters is as valuable as having sons, though in some areas they think that daughters are better, and girls are educated in their traditions by grandmothers (Cheng 1993; Du 1991: 417).

Maternal uncles play important roles in Jino marriages and are often asked to preside over weddings and divorce ceremonies. When a couple gets married, a bowl is smashed and a maternal uncle keeps the broken pieces. If the couple wants to divorce, the uncle throws away the pieces of the bowl and pours two cups of wine on the ground (Ye 1993).

A wedding will usually lasts for three days, but it cannot be celebrated on the bride's birthday or on a date with a seven in it, because as women have seven souls seven is not considered propitious (Zhao 1995: 18). On the first day the family of the

74

groom will go to the bride's family. The following day, the groom and his parents go to escort the bride home, there the groom gives a certain amount of money to the bride's mother and uncle. A hog is slaughtered at the bride's home as an offering to the ancestors. The hog's head and feet are given to the village elders and a big chunk of meat is given to the bride's father (Ye 1993: 152; Du 1991: 414).

After eating, the bride has her teeth blackened with rosewood sap; she is then led out of her parent's home. As she leaves her village her former boyfriends take revenge by splashing water on her. On arrival at the groom's home she is welcomed with clean water, and she is given an egg (symbol of the happiness that the new wedding brings to the family) by her mother in law, who then performs the "thread fastening" ceremony by coiling a red thread around the young woman's wrists three times. Her wrists are also wrapped with red thread by her father-in-law and other elders. The thread is considered an auspicious protection against evil spirits and symbolizes the bride's real "ties" with the family. Early next morning she must go to fetch water from the village well, offering her parents in law warm water for washing their faces. From that moment on she calls them "father" and "mother" (Ye 1993: 152-3).

One of the main aims of the wedding ceremony is to carry the soul, spirit, energy and the meat of the bride to the bridegroom's house, to accept that the name of her children will follow the name of her husband. As soon as the bride arrives at the groom's house there are some ceremonies carried out which fix her there. Her bone, however, remains with her uncle, meaning that she keeps an important link with her house, which will be used in case of divorce (Du 2008: 181).

Once a formal marriage has taken place, both husband and wife are expected to remain faithful to each other. The husband cannot have sexual relations out of wedlock. If he did so, the wife can leave their home taking with her all the gifts received at the wedding (Zhong 1983; Du 1991: 414). The husband is the head of the family and enjoys a higher position inside it. But the wife is not discriminated against and her role is higher in some social, productive, ritual and homely matters. Though the wife moves to her husband's house she is not separated from her own family, since people marry from inside the village. A piece of cloth symbolizes the equal position of women in the family. If a woman discovers that her husband has violated the marriage customs, it suffices to cut the cloth as a sign that the marriage has ended. When a couple divorces, the children usually remain with the mother (Du 1991: 415).

In their daily life there are vestiges of their former matriarchal society, as the proverbs show: "mother runs the house" or "only the mother has the right to sacrifice hens to give its soul to the sick children." This is a remnant of the traditional power of the female elders' council in the matriarchal times. The elevated status of women at home existed long ago. They often say Abu Pila and Amo Pile. Abu means father, and Pila means a host that is often out, while Amo means mother, and Pile means hostess at home. "In the past, when children fell ill, a shaman would be invited to dispel evil spirits. Traditionally, mothers must be at home in order for the ritual to be effective because only mothers had the right to "tie up the souls" of the children (Zhao 1995: 21; Du 1991: 409).

Love between people that belong to the same clan is common among the Jino. There are several stories that emphasize the romantic side of this love, usually forbidden. Maybe the past prevalence of marriage among the young of the same family meant that when the rule that they cannot marry with people from the same clan was established, severe punishments faced those who broke this taboo. To compensate for the hard treatment that those engaged in physical love with people of the same clan will suffer, their spiritual romantic engagement is highly praised. When two people of the same clan fall in love but do not marry they are highly admired and allowed to express their affection even after death. This is called the Bashi love. They want to be together after death and go together to their ancestors' realm, since they cannot express their love in this world. During their lifetime they express their love changing gifts. When one of them dies, the other puts all these gifts beside his or her corpse (Du 1991: 416).

Death and funeral.

The Jino hold the elderly in great respect. Old people, due to their age, occupy the most important political and ritual positions in the family and the village. Respect for one's elders continues even after their death; when a complex set of ceremonies exists to guarantee their well being in the land of the shadows.

In the funeral customs of the Jino many rituals seem closely related to those performed in Old China. Some of them don't seem to be related to Chinese local traditions but rather to traditions that were common in China 2,000 years ago, and even older. These data could suggest that the legends relating the origin of the Jino with the lost soldiers of Zhuge Liang could have an historical basis, and that the Chinese influence on Jino funeral customs happened 1,800 years ago. It is possible that a detailed comparison of other aspects of Jino traditional culture with Chinese culture in the Han dynasty could give light to new understanding of some of the characteristics of the Jino and Chinese culture.

If somebody dies in the morning they bury him in the afternoon, if he dies in the afternoon, he must be buried the following day (Zhu 2009: 85). When somebody dies they put an egg in his hand and two coins over his eyes, and arrange beside the corpse the tools and clothes that he used when he was alive, sometimes then buried with him as sacrificial objects. Old Chinese traditions show that this practice was common in China more than 2,000 years ago, now substituted with the internment of the dead with cheap objects specifically made to be buried. If the deceased is old a fan and a cloth is added to protect him against hot and cold weather.

After the dead of the father, sons express their mourning by taking out their caps and personal ornaments and the married daughters change their hair-style and comb their hair with a filial bun. Then they perform the ceremony of unrolling the cloth. This cloth, arranged in advance, is rolled around a piece of wood. The sons and daughters of the deceased climb to the roof of the house, while other relatives and neighbors wait below watching them. They allow the cloth to unroll from the roof until it reaches the ground. If the cloth unrolls smoothly it means that sons and daughters are filial. This ritual presents a considerable psychological strain on the sons and daughters, as it is a public probe of their filial love (Cheng 1993: 59)

Later, sons and daughters are reverential before the corpse, whilst praying:

"Father (mother), you left us.
You are going to the place where the spirits live.
You must protect to the old and young people in your family,

that all matters are successful
To get money doing business
A good harvest when we crop grains
A good hunt when we go to the mountain." (Cheng 1993)

Each son hangs a bamboo tube in the beam of the house, whose content is checked three times every day. If they find things inside that resemble grains it is considered a sign of good harvest; if they find some animal hairs, it means they will have a good hunt; but if there is nothing they consider it a bad portend (Cheng 1993).

They use a tree trunk as a coffin, sometimes chosen by the deceased before his death, or sometimes fell after the death actually happens. This is a custom again that may be related with old Chinese tradition, as we know that "In ancient times, when the Emperor Yao was buried, they used a hollow tree for a coffin" (Groot, 1: 309). Poor people use some wood planks or a bamboo coffin. The coffin must be made of wood or bamboo, to allow the soul to sail across the rivers that he will find on his way to the ancestral lands (Zheng 2008: 152).

They dance a funeral dance before the coffin called the "Painted face and the bamboo poles", where one person paints his face with ashes and blood to resemble a spirit and four people move their bamboo poles as if defending the corpse from being eaten by this evil spirit. They perform the ceremony of beating the demons, where men enter the dark forest with their heads covered with bamboo masks. On the way to the burial site they spread grain and shoot their guns to frighten evil spirits. The procession is opened by some people carrying flags, sometimes cut in the shapes of human beings, horses, or chickens. Relatives follow them dressed in white clothes. Two people blowing the *suona* open the way for the soul of the deceased, because he must choose the correct way in the nine cross-roads that he will find. Six offerings of meat inside a bamboo tube will be buried with him to be given to the spirits that protect the six main gates he must cross along his way (Cheng 1993).

Each village has a cemetery where dead people must be buried. After burying a deceased person a dog is sacrificed and also buried in the coffin because they think that the dog can lead the soul in the world of the shadows. The role of the dog as psychopomp is suggested in some Han dynasty tombs, where clay dogs, sometimes of considerable size, have been unearthed. A small bamboo house is built over the grave with some sticks making a fence around it, in which the family of the dead places offerings of food daily, sometimes for as long as two or three years (Zhi 1984: 90). One custom that relates them again to old Chinese culture, as we know that the ancient Chinese supplied a sumptuous meal the day the dead man was dressed for the grave and that the nobility and gentry went so far as to continue the process of feeding after the coffining, by placing baskets with scorched grain and dried fish and meat inside the wooden shed in which the body was stored away in the hall of the mansion (Groot, I: 360).

Before leaving the burial site they smear the fence with the blood of the dog, and leave a gate open for the people to enter. They believe that in the past there were savage people who fed on their dead. The blood of the dog is used to make them believe that the corpse has been already eaten. Then the people close the door of the fence, and the family kowtows as a farewell. In their way back home and before leaving the burial ground all their footprints must be erased in order to avoid the bad spirits to follow them. Before entering their house again they wash their hands carefully to avoid dirty things and evil spirits which could harm them (Cheng 1993).

During the funeral it is customary for other people living in the same village to give some gifts to the family of the deceased. When the family comes back from the cemetery an old man must give them some eggs and must tie a white thread on the wrist of each person (left wrist for men and right for women), symbolizing that he is tying their soul to their bodies to prevent their souls following the deceased's soul in a moment of weakness. If after the death of a person in the family they make a new house, they must go to the burial site to invite the deceased to the new house (Cheng 1993).

Zhuoba and zhuosheng funerals are much more solemn occasions, with all the people of the village stopping work for a day and a ritual moving of the drum from the house of the deceased leader to that of the new leader. Sadness and joy are mixed in this day; while one family mourns his dead parent, the other enjoys their chance to have the drum (Cheng 1993).

In Yanuo village one year after the death they carry out the ceremony to take the deceased's soul to their original land, where they arrange some offerings in the house of the zhuoba and ask the bailapao to send the deceased's soul to the ancestors' land. To do this he names the main places in the soul's way to prevent his getting lost (Cheng 1993).

Abnormal deaths are treated in special ways. The corpse of women that die in a difficult delivery of a child are burned or put on a platform for a wind burial, letting it to get rotten by the wind, sun and rain. Men that die by a snake bite, by cause of water, poisonous beasts or before reaching age are buried in any place.

81

Hunters believed that they must be buried with their guns, since only a man with a gun could find the right way in the other world. After the hunting ban in Jino lands in 1997, and the requisition of their guns, some Jino men made new weapons, not to hunt, but to be used ritually in their funerals (Wang 2004).

Chapter 5

Yearly festivals and rituals.

The ritual yearly cycle of the Jino consisted of two main festivals and a series of minor rituals related to the different phases of their agricultural production. The two main festivals were Luomaluo or Worship the Goddess Festival, and Temaoke or Forging-Iron Festival. The first was a sad festival commemorating the death of their goddess Amoyaobai, the second was a happy celebration in which hopes were focused on the coming start of the production activities. They may also have calendrical connections which are now lost, as the first is celebrated in the seventh lunar month and the second in the first lunar month. In both them the protagonist is a goddess, Amoyaobai's sad funeral, and The Goddess of the Iron-smith in Temaoke. Nowadays most Jino villages only celebrate Temaoke, whose length and intensity varies from one village to the other.

Temaoke Festival

Temaoke or Forging-Iron Festival is the New Year for the Jino. It is an old ceremony traditionally held prior to sowing in February, but there is not a fixed date and the various branches and villages of the Jino celebrate it on different days. Under normal circumstances, the elders of each village would determine the specific time for celebrating the festival on the basis of two factors: first, according to their knowledge of seasonal changes in the natural environment and the auspiciousness of different days as shown by divination, and second, according to the relative position of each village on the Jino Mountain. As has already been explained the Aha and Axi branches distinguish between parents' and children's villages, children's villages cannot celebrate the festival before their parents' villages (Zhu 2009). Now, Temaoke Festival begins on February 6th in the administrative center of Jino Township, celebrated in the following days by the parents' villages, and in near dates by the children villages, not always after the parents' villages. Basa Village celebrates on Feb 1st.

The asynchrony in the celebration of the festival was a main tool for enhancing ethnic consciousness among the Jino and forging a kind of ethnic unity among the villages, as celebrations promoted visits between members of different villages as well as ritual interchanges between parent and children villages. Inter-village relations were promoted, with elders from different villages visiting each other during these days, exchanging gifts and festive meals. It is a relaxed opportunity to discuss possible problems which may emerge during the year and to promote a peaceful and harmonious coexistence between the clans and villages.

Temaoke festival has elements in common New Year celebrations of around China, such as ceremonies of bidding farewell to the old year and welcoming the new, but here the most important role is that of the blacksmiths, respected by everyone because they could divine peoples' fortunes through dream interpretation and also make iron tools for the villagers. The blacksmith is one of the most important offices in Jino villages, as their swidden agriculture relies heavily on their iron knives and axes. Iron tools (of which they use eight kinds) play a central role in the felling of trees, opening new fields, and with the yearly labor that takes place within them. Iron, coming from outside, replaced stone, wood and bamboo tools among the Jino. With the use of iron tools their productivity increased to a level that allowed them to sustainably use their natural resources for extended periods of time (Yin 2001; Zhu: 2009).

The origin of this festival in told in a legend that says once a Jino woman was pregnant for nine years with no childbirth. Sorcerers could not help her, until one day she suddenly felt an acute pain in her belly, and her child, a sturdy boy, broke seven of her ribs and jumped out himself. With a pair of tongs in his left hand and a hammer in his right one, the child immediately began to do the blacksmith's work and produced all sorts of iron tools. He is considered the ancestor and teacher of Jino blacksmiths (Zhu 2009: 4). In each Jino village there are usually some blacksmiths. Before the New Year the zhuoba will choose one of them to represent the village and to have dreams for the entire village.

Before the beginning of the festival they must make offerings to the Goddess of the Blacksmiths, praying to her to give good dreams to the blacksmith and to expel the evil spirits. Then they would arrange all the objects needed, including images of Mahei and Maniu, and the animals that would be offered to the drum. Drums, drumsticks, iron-smith's tools, and cymbals must be washed and prepared, as well as *daluo* to drive away evil spirits, and their games and musical instruments as the *chik*, the most special of them (Zhu 2009: 20-8). "Thinking that the drum saved their ancestors, the Jino see it as a holy object and have it preserved in the zhuoba' house in normal times. When it is to be beat for New Year celebration, it should first be offered a sacrifice and adorned with multicolored flowers" (He: 2005: 284).

In the first day the most important sacrificial rite is held in the house of the blacksmith. In the ceremonial prayer, the blacksmith is referred to as a giant who has a hammer in his right hand and a pair of tongs in his left, exercising immense power to control rivers and seas, and to fasten the doors of demons by driving in a golden nail. On New Year's Eve he is requested to have a good dream in the night. On the morning of the New Year, he is invited by the zhuoba to his home and seated in the seat of honor. The zhuoba ask him about his dreams from last night. They believe that by interpreting his dreams they can tell whether the year's harvest will be good or bad. Later they designate two helpers to the blacksmith, as well as potential new blacksmiths (Deng and Zhang 1991: 137; Zhu 2009: 39).

Next they perform the ox-slaughtering ceremony, when villagers first tie up an ox's four limbs, then a young man chops off the animal's rear legs, cuts from its bottom a piece of meat as sacrificial offering, and finally distributes all the meat to the villagers. Then the people pay their respects to the elders and offer them some gifts. The drum is taken out of the zhuoba's house, and is carefully washed. They worship to the big drum while the myth of the origin of the drum is repeated. The beating of the drum represents the beginning of the New Year. In some places a woman beats the wooden drum, men dance around it and women dance in an outer circle. Be it to expel evil spirits or to express joy, Temaoke is a festival of singing and dancing. After dancing and singing before the drum, a communal banquet takes place, in which everyone eats together, and the zhuoba and the elders sing the songs of the New Year, the content of which refers to their traditions (Zhu 2009: 99).

In the second day they worship to the Goddess of the Blacksmith and all the families' heads attend a ceremony to symbolically forge iron to make farm tools for the spring ploughing. Then they repair the iron tools and worship at home to each family's ancestors. They believe that the new iron tools made in the festival will bring them good luck in farming and in the subsequent harvest. On the third day, after a ritual iron casting, the villagers, led by the elders, repair roads and demarcate boundary lines of the clan and the village fields (Zhu 2009; He 2005: 238). In some villages the festival ends with Gazhuli rituals, whose meaning is to discard the old and welcome the new. A group of young men dressed in shabby clothes and tree-bark clothes, face blackened, dance around the village between two rows of girls, following the big drum in a comic way. Arriving at the village square they change new clothes to symbolize the arrival of the New Year (Zhu 2009: 92).

After Temaoke Festival the people and their tools are ready for the agricultural activities that lie ahead. The end of the New Year celebration is the Ceremony of Sowing, when they gather in the house of the blacksmith, and the zhuoba prays for a good harvest and ritually sows some seeds near the house, the people following him. Then the people sacrifice an ox that will be offered to zhuoba and the blacksmith, and to the spirits on the road, and its meat is shared by everybody. When they finish the banquet the people dance until nighttime (Cheng 1993: 106).

Nowadays the festival lasts for only one day. The blacksmith has lost his importance but not the drum, whose spirit receives the homage of the people before announcing the New Year. The elders, headed by the zhuoba, offer the head of a pig to the spirit of the drum, praying for a good harvest the coming

87

year while throwing some grains of rice at the drum and towards heaven in the hope that by means of sympathetic magic, grain will be provided for them in the future.

Luomaluo or the Goddess Festival

Luomaluo or the Festival to Worship the Goddess commemorates the death of the ancestor Amoyaobai, the great goddess. It is not a happy festival but a sad one and the village is thus closed. It is celebrated on the seventh month. It starts on a dragon day and it is sometimes called the Dragon Festival or Worship the Dragon, and could be related to the worship of the protector of the village, common among other ethnic groups in the area. The night before the zhuoba makes an announcement that during the thirteen days (the time Amoyaobai spent creating the world) that this festival lasts for people cannot sing, dance or play musical instruments. Her funeral also lasted thirteen days. Each day has some activities which are to be performed. The first day they block the roads to the village and the village is cleaned. The second day they sacrifice a cow under a tree that is offered to the Deity of the Village, and its meat is shared equally among all the families. On the third day people pay their respects to other people in the village, with younger brothers worshiping ancestors in the older brothers' houses. On the fourth day old folks pay their respects to the zhuoba, on the fifth the elders discuss the ritual calendar for the next year. On the sixth day production activities are allowed and women busy themselves grinding rice grains. If during the time of this festival somebody dies they must be buried quickly without much ceremony (or not buried at all) and their relatives cannot cry for them (Yu 2000: 140).

The seventh day, the dog day, is the most solemn day, when nobody can work. The zhuoba and zhuosheng hang two daliu on the gates of the village. Nobody can enter or leave the village. They arrange seven tables in the zhuoba's house, where the seven elders sit reciting their prayers. Later, a pig is killed in the zhuosheng's house and its meat is divided among all the people. The zhuoba prays to the village god to protect them against the bad spirits. Then they can go on with their daily activities, though it is still prohibited to sing and dance, and to grind grain for several more days, when the zhuoba is supposed to be dealing with the spirits, then the festival ends. Each day of the Jino horoscope commemorates the process of the death of Amoyaobai. and is remembered as such in the festival. The last day, rooster day, is celebrated as the moment when she was burned and ascended heaven (Du 1996: 880; Yu 2000).

Nowadays this festival is no longer celebrated, and in the few villages that do, it usually lasts only three days. The village is closed. Under a tree near the village they sacrifice a cow, and a mother pig and seven piglets near the pond, the heads of all these animals hanging near the place of sacrifice. On the second day the people eat together in the house of the zhuoba. On the third, the village is completely closed and all activity stops. These days people remember their myths and traditions, and this ceremony provides a good moment for the people to enhance their ethnic conscience (Cheng 1993: 115).

Rituals that accompany agricultural activities

The Jino year is marked by ceremonies that accompany the process of agricultural work requiring the help of different deities for their successful development. Ceremonies that make agriculture a sacred activity are needed for the survival of the people, as an expression of their hopes for a rich harvest.

Their ritual life, not exactly the same in all villages, was so complex and full of meaning that they have a kind of guide map to their yearly rituals, known as *Puzhuzi*. This is a poem chanted to remember the exact time and the way in which their most important ritual activities must be done during the year. It begins by telling that the New Year ended and that the time of working in the fields is beginning. The elders' council must gather to choose the proper time to start work. It reminds the people that the tools must be repaired and properly arranged, and the way in which they must arrange the fields with the firebreaks before burning them. It then describes all the yearly activities and the rituals that must accompany them in chronological order (Committee 1996).

In the first month they allocate the lands to be used by the different clans of the village, and the people mark their land's boundaries with some wood swords or other signs. Ceremonies are directed to the spirit of the pond of the village and to the spirit of the village, asking for safety and prosperity in the coming year, and ginger, taro and daliu are scattered around the allotted fields to prevent the presence of evil spirits. They carry out small rituals that accompany the preparatory labors in the fields, such as the Ritual of making the holes or the Ritual of the felling of the forest, when the zhuoba and the zhuosheng symbolically fell several trees as a prelude to tree felling activities. Miaojieruo is the end of tree-felling ritual, at which point the zhuoba and zhuosheng ritually end this activity (Yin 2001, Yu 2000: 140).

The first of their main agricultural ceremonies is Kebiterou. It is a drum ritual celebrated by the elders of the village lead by the zhuoba and zhuosheng announcing that they are ready for cultivation. It must be celebrated on exactly the 13th day of the year before sunrise. They arrange some offerings on a table to the Deity of the Village in the house of the zhuoba, around which the elders sit. Then the zhuoba must inform this deity that according to their tradition they are beginning their agricultural work, and before it, they offer a sacrifice to him asking her help in protecting the village, the elders and the fields. They bury ginger and taro to expel evil spirits and hang two *daliu* for the same purpose. Then zhuoba and zhuosheng separate, each going to a different place to cut two small trees and putting them at the side of the two main roads that lead to the village. This is a ritual enactment of the works that the rest of the people of the village will soon start (Du 1996: 800, Yin 2001; XSNB 1989: 134).

The ceremony of burning the fields is held at around the end of February or the beginning of March. The council of elders gathers in the zhuoba's house to inform the Village Deity about their coming activities and to ask for her protection. During this prayer the way they will do their different works is explained in minute detail, with the aim of remembering that all must be done according to tradition, as well as to the contents of this tradition. They carry out a ceremony asking the spirit of land, tree, bush and wind for a successful burn. When the prayer is finished they go to the fields and do as stated. A dog is sacrificed in order to drive away evil spirits, and a chicken is offered to the wind deity. They make a firebreak and start to burn from the top of the mountain downwards. Men usually burn the trees with torches while women have water ready to avoid the propagation of fire. When they burn the fields care must be taken to burn only the desired field and to prevent the fire getting out of control. When they burn the field they have a witness from another village, who oversees that they make the firebreak properly, that they perform the correct ceremonies, that they not trespass their field boundaries, and that in the case of the fire extending beyond the firebreak he can exempt of responsibility to the party in which field the fire originated (Du 1996: 803; Yu 2000: 140).

During the middle of the third month they raise small huts where they will rest while working in the fields. This must be done with the corresponding ceremony called Dongburou or building the field huts ritual, in which the spirits of the land are prayed for protection against harm. Zhuoba and zhuosheng raise their huts, and after them every family must raise their hut, and must recite a prayer which depicts in detail how they must build their new huts (Du 1996: 803, Yu 2000: 140, Yin 2001).

Before sowing the seed the Jino carry out a ceremony to call the Deity of Grain, where the women of each family go the fields to sow the grain, and go back home. Then the main woman of each family, dressed in their best attire, meet at a cross-road where they will call the Deity of Grain together. When they finish this ritual call they go back home, where each family sacrifices a chicken that will be offered, with wine, rice, and tea to the grain deity while they pray for have enough food for the coming year (Eorc- 87).

In the fourth month they celebrate the sowing the grain ceremony, which lasts two days and has two main rituals. On the first day they sacrifice an ox, whose meat will be shared evenly with best portions going to the elders, and offered by the zhuoba to the Deity of the Village, Deity of the Pond, Deity of the Grains and Deity of the Mountains as well as to the spirit of his deceased father and mother, asking them to protect their crops from pest and rodents, birds, flooding and other calamities, and for a good harvest. The following day each family will sow their own fields, but before they start they must sow the fields of the seven elders, and carry out some short rituals including the sacrifice of a chicken, whose blood and entrails are smeared on some previously erected wooden sticks about two meters high, the burying of taro and ginger, and the hanging of daliu to expel evil spirits. Then the family of the younger brother helps the older brother, and the following day the older will help the younger. It ends with a prayer to the Deity of Grain asking her that the grain they planted may multiply (Du 1996: 805; Eorc-111).

The worship heaven ceremony was formerly held on May 24th but now it is celebrated in Temaoke festival. Presided over by the zhuoba and the elders, offerings are put on a place where lightning struck and prayers are conveyed to the god, asking for good luck and prosperity: good harvest, health for the people and their animals, and good luck fishing and hunting. With the meaning related to their traditional agriculture lost, this ritual is held at other time, and sometimes even on a dance stage (Zhu 2009: 90).

The Torch Festival is celebrated around the 24th of the sixth month. On this night, amongst the sound of gongs, whistles and songs, all the people in the village, men and women, old and young, carry small torches and gather in the square, where a big torch is burning. Some of the younger villagers climb a tree and they throw food to the rest of the people from one of its high branches. They then sing and dance the whole night.

On the sixth month the open the gate ceremony marks the beginning of the hunting season. This same month they usually perform the Cutou ceremony to worship the Mother Thunder Youmomizhe, an ancestral mother that according to their traditions lives in heaven grinding rice. If her grinding stone moves quickly or it is placed upside down, thunder surges and the human beings on the earth can be hit be a lightning. As Jino villages are usually hit by lightning they ask the bailapao to perform this ceremony to this goddess, and present some offerings to her (Eorc. 795).

The ceremony to Eat the New Rice or Haoxizao is celebrated at the end of the seventh or the beginning of the eighth lunar months, when the rice is nearly ripe. This is a festival related to the dogs that brought cereals to the human beings, and dogs are fed every night by the Jino before they go to sleep. Each family can choose the time to celebrate it, but it must be after the zhuoba and zhuosheng have done it. In the morning women go to the fields and take home some rice, pepper and about 10 kinds of currently ripe vegetables. They must sacrifice three chickens, one to the deceased father and mother, one to the spirit of the village and one to the spirit of grain. They pray for good luck in the coming days, when they will be busy harvesting the grain. A large amount of chicken is eaten as it is customary to host the whole village with choice offerings from their fields. While they are steaming rice they examine the direction in which the steam comes out. To the east foretells offspring prosperity, to the south a bumper harvest, to the west abundant hunt, and to the north symbolizes misfortune (Song 2007; Yin 200; Du 1996: 818).

Gusakuluoku or calling the soul of the rice to come with them back to the storehouses. It is celebrated in the tenth lunar month, when the grain is stored in the granary. Each family, after the leaders, performs this themselves. They go to the field with the offering of a chicken and call the spirit of the grain to come back home, rather than stay in the fields. They offer a pig before the granary to the deceased father and mother, the Deity of the Village and the Deity of the Grain (Du 1996: 819).

At the end of the agricultural cycle, in the dry months of September, October and November the people repair their houses or build new ones.

Chapter 6

Material Culture of the Jino.

Swidden agriculture

The Jino believe that mother earth is not only the abode of their main goddesses but also the place from where, thanks to these goddesses, they get shelter, food and clothes to sustain their life. The relationship between the Jino and Mother Earth is based on a deep respect and a thorough knowledge of her qualities. The respect is shown in the ceremonies we will see in chapter 6. Here we will show the Jino knowledge of their environment.

The main traditional economic activities of the Jino were slash and burn agriculture, gathering of forest products and hunting; they raised also some domestic animals, especially pigs and chickens; fishing being important for some communities. Nowadays they crop rice and corn for their sustenance, but rubber, tea, ornamental flowers and medicinal plants are more and more important to their livelihood. During centuries of agricultural work in poor mountainous lands they developed techniques that allowed them an optimal use of the natural resources. Slash and burn agriculture combined a surprising knowledge of the quality of soils, and the specific climatic conditions of different areas in a single field, with the use of a high number of rice varieties and intercropping with other vegetal species. The result was a successful environmental protection that allowed, for a long term, productivity of their lands guaranteeing the continuous supply of their staple food and the integration of agriculture and hunting and gathering.

In each village there are strict rules to choose which land will be slashed and burned to avoid the deforestation of a large area and to prevent fire disaster effectively. To do it they have divided the different environments according to their characteristics, and established the kind of economic activities that can be done in each of them. For instance they divide between Oukou Oukoumiu, or forests on the mountain top, that cannot be cut, Oukoulou, or forest on the ridge, Oukoulou Acelie or forests on the mountainside, used for fruit-collecting, forest used for hunting, etc.

Based on differences in the natural properties of the land, the Jino distinguish three categories: *zhexiao* or low altitude land, which is the land under a regime of fallow; *dieta* or high altitude land with poorer soils, and *zhejiao* or medium altitude land; occupying these three kinds of land a 30%, 30% and 40% of their total cultivable area respectively. This classification, found by geologists to be rather scientific, served to them to deploy methods of cultivation best suited for each category. The *dieta* land was cultivated for just one season, after which the land was left fallow. Most villages divided this type of land into thirteen sections, and cultivate one each year with an ensuing fallow of thirteen years to guarantee a healthy re-growth, the number thirteen originated from the legend that Amoyaobai was buried on the thirteen day after her death. *Zhejiao* land is cultivated for two or three years and is left fallow for 15 years or more. *Zhexiao* land is continuously used for up to ten years, the fallow needed for a complete recovery of the soil last for more than 20 years (Yin 2001: 230-8).

They use different cultivation techniques for different categories of land. The complex ways in which they combine hill rice varieties take into account the general altitude, slope gradient, and differences in temperature between the higher and lower part of a field, etc. This means that even within a relatively small area large numbers of rice varieties may be used. To balance the need for food and the sustainable use of the land, besides the use of different rice varieties, they use cotton to enrich the soil, they rotate crops with grass and seeds, and they use the called "field of a hundred treasures", where all kinds of crops are simultaneously cultivated. "The highly sophisticated techniques for continuous cultivation over several consecutive seasons are one of the outstanding characteristics of Jino swidden agriculture" (Yin 2001: 245-252).

The crops cultivated by the Jino include hill rice, maize, sorghum, and *su* millet. In the past cotton was the major source of raw material for clothing, and was also used to exchange for salt, iron tools, and other goods with the outside world, and for payment of taxes and tributes to the Dai chieftains. Nowadays in some villages it is still woven to make their traditional clothes. Other cash crops were tea, famous in the rest of China for centuries, tobacco and oil plants, such as peanuts and sesame seeds (Yin 2001: 241).

In the whole Jino territory more than 100 varieties of rice have been found. Only in Baya village 38 varieties of rice are found. Some traditional rice varieties have been already lost, others are now scarcely used. Of the seventy-one varieties used in the 1990s sixteen were early-ripening varieties, thirty-five were medium-ripening, twenty late-ripening, and twenty-five sticky or glutinous varieties. To choose the kind of rice to plant in each plot of land they consider not only specific soil conditions, humidity and microclimatic variations, but they include an overall assessment of all the cultivable land to deploy different kinds of early-medium-and-late-ripening varieties to guarantee a continuous supply of grain and to avoid seasonal shortages (Yin 2001).

In swidden agriculture it is essential to pay attention to the seasons. The Jino have their own calendar, preserved in the old *Puzhizi* songs dealing with the farming seasons, which divides the year into eleven months, and each month into thirty days. To ascertain the proper season for each of the agricultural activities they rely also on natural signs, such as the call of particular birds or the blossoming of particular kinds of flowers. Different agricultural activities are timed to reduce the amount of weeds. The sowing time is decided with reference to the topography, altitude, soil fertility, etc. (Yin 2001: 258). Although their laboring methods are rather primitive, their knowledge of their environment provided them with yields that are favorably compared to those of more developed ethnic groups living near them (Du 1991: 408).

Gathering activities

The vast areas of forest and fallow land provided ample resources for gathering, especially important in the season when there was a shortage of grain. They usually gathered from forest lands and swidden fields nearby. Near 200 species of edible plants have been identified among the Jino, with 86 species of wild vegetables and 37 species of wild fruits (Wang and Long). More specific studies confirm that they gather 11 kinds of tubers, 40 wild herbs and vegetables, 12 kinds of bamboo shoots, 15 kinds of mushrooms, and 24 different fruits. It is important to note that each of these vegetable

99

species is used for different reasons and prepared in a different way (Yin 2001: 440). They gather 23 insect species as food, which are believed to be helpful for pest control, and they collect and use also about 60 ~ 70 plant species for medicinal purposes (Long et al).

To guarantee a continuous supply of non timber forest products the preservation of the forest is of paramount importance. They have a quasi-scientific knowledge of the characteristics of their forest. Near the villages, up above the mountain, they preserve usually a sacred forest, where some spirits abode. Most of their community forests were traditionally classified according to its perceived function before Jino eyes. They have watershed forest to protect against torrential rains, auspicious forest considered the abode of spirits and deities, sacred forest around the villages as a kind of buffer zone between the wild world outside and the civilized world of the village, boundary forest that separate the territories of contiguous clans or villages, fire protection forest, burial forest and swidden fallow forest. Every type of forest was managed through traditional regulations. The village headmen were in charge of implementing the traditional management system. Because it was popular with local villagers and also because there was a strict punishment of offenders, the management system was effective (Long and Zhou).

Swidden agriculture maintains a higher diversity of crops and secondary vegetation than other sedentary farming techniques. Swidden farming enhances biodiversity and forest regeneration by means of protection of useful species in swidden-fallow fields, combining local annual crops and perennial tree crops, and domesticating native plants (Fu 2005: 365).

Hunting

For highland peoples hunting was as indispensable as gathering and sometimes even more important. The Jino are great hunters. Researches taken place in an average Jino village (Baka) showed that in 1987 father and son hunting expeditions yielded ten large game animals a year, as well as many smaller animals caught in spring traps, sometimes as many as ten a day. When men went out hunting, they shouldered crossbows with poisoned arrows or shot-guns. They were also experts in the use of traps and nooses to catch wild animals. In their well forested mountains, a rich animal variety was found, including more than 100 species of mammals, 420 of birds, 36 amphibious, 60 of reptiles and more than 100 kinds of fishes. The Jino divided the game animals in birds, rats and beasts.

Traditionally they practiced two types of hunting, one was aimed at capturing wild animals, and the other aimed at protecting their crops from ravages caused by wild animals and birds. Hunting expeditions varied in size and duration. In some of the biggest hunting expeditions, especially those carried on in the second and third month, after burning the fields, all the village people, took advantage of the fact that the animals were running in every direction scared by the fires, to leave the village in their pursuit. Near the harvest, when the grains were almost ripe, they kept hunting in order to stop wild animals eating their grains. There were individual hunting expeditions and groups, usually of people belonging to different families, hunting together. Men sometimes changed their cap for hunting expeditions, trying to pass as wild animals (Yin 2001: 453).

After hunting big game they needed to make sacrifices to the Goddess of Hunt, usually offering her the ears of the animal, while praying: "Goddess of Hunt, goddess of the mountain, I hunted an animal that was yours. It's not I who caught it; it is you who gave it to me. We will eat it together, we will enjoy it together" (Cheng 1993: 76). If the game was scarce or the hunting expeditions were not successful they held a ceremony for the goddess. They made a sedan with banana leaves and put inside clay figurines of chicken, pigs, deer, wild-ox, horses, which were to be brought before the village deity. Elders prayed asking the village deity to expel evil spirits that made it difficult to hunt, and invited the game and mountain spirits to help them. The people danced in their own houses with wooden swords to expel evil spirits. The ceremony ended with the people carrying the sedan with all the figurines out of the village in a procession shouting their will to hunt animals (Cheng 1993).

When they catch an animal they preserved a part of its body, such as the horns or the claws, as an offering to the incumbent deity and as a probe of the ability of the hunter. Coming back to the village from a hunting trip the hunters made a *chik* with seven bamboo tubes of different lengths and beat it while singing. Listening to their rhythm the people could know how big the catch was. If they got a big game, when they approached the village singing, their relatives left the village to join them in singing the hunting song. Some small ceremonies were performed and a feast celebrated to invite the rest of the people in the village, and to appease the spirits (Yu 2000: 48).

While small game and birds were usually eaten by the hunter family, the big game must be shared. Sometimes the hunter who caught it received a leg and the skin, and the rest of the meat was divided more or less evenly between the families of the village. Other times the foreleg was reserved for the oldest man in the village (Zhong 1983). "Even a small deer is cut into very tiny pieces and shared out among all the villagers, including new-borns" (Ma 1989).

Protective hunting was undertaken to limit the damage wild animals did to crops. In these hunting expeditions the protection of the fields was as important as the game animals caught. Sometimes they consisted in joyous excursions in which a large number of villagers gathered to drive away the animals that might otherwise trample the crops. Just before the autumn harvest, when the grains are almost ripe and the damage the animals can cause is the most dangerous for Jino survival, many families spent the whole day in their fields, sleeping by turns in the small huts built near them. They guarded and patrolled their fields night and day, so to shoot birds and other animals that use to eat the crops. In 1958 authorities calculated that in the whole Jino district people set up 18.080 traps and dug 68,900 pitfalls in the fall of the year, and that in this way they caught 964 deer and wild boars, and 14,558 mountain rodents (Yin 2001: 460-1).

Fishing is especially important among the Jino of the Buyuan branch, as the big Xiaohei and Mengwang rivers cross their territory. They usually dry the fish and preserve them in big jars (Yu 2000: 48).

Jino villages and their leaders: the mothers of the village.

The Jino live in about 40 villages organized around consanguineous clans. There are one or more clans in each village. Membership in clans is passed down from a father to his children, just as the membership in the lineage groups which make up each clan (West 2009: 349). Each village was a small, self-contained world. Land was communally owned by clans or villages and farmed collectively, with clear boundaries between the lands belonging to different clans, sometimes marked with special features of the landscape or with arrows and swords arranged on a platform. Besides the lands belonging to the clans, some tracts of land were considered village property and its products were used to pay tributes and taxes demanded by the local authorities. There was no private ownership of the land until the 20th century and before the modern changes never became very important (Yin 2001: 228).

Villages are for the Jino the territory of humans per excellence, as opposed to the wild exterior landscapes where spirits possibly dangerous inhabit. Villages were established in mythical times by their ancestors, ancestral mothers usually, that thanks to their outstanding powers and spiritual qualities, acquired for themselves and their offspring the right to inhabit lands formerly populated by hostile spirits. Founding mothers were later deified as village deities, and their spirit said to inhabit the village deity pillar, from where they extended their protection to their offspring, and where they are worshipped in their main ceremonies or during difficult situations. Each village has its own deity, symbolized by the drum, which in this way represents the village. Each village has its own cultural characteristics: language and dress, buildings, production, leadership, and yearly ceremonies, are all slightly different (Zheng 2008: 4).

Because the village is the place where people feel protected from outside evil spirits it has some buildings of religious or ritual relevance. The three most important are: the spirits gate, the village deity pillar and the pond. The spirit gate is possibly the most important, as it separates the territory of people, opposed to the outside territory of the spirits. Usually it has a *daliu* hanging from it, as a sign that the territory is protected from evil spirits. The pole of the Village Deity stands in the sunlight near the houses of the people; it is considered a sacred pole where the leaders perform sacrificial ceremonies to the Village Deity. Every family must hang some blade bones of animals in this pole. In each village there is a pond. When they suffer from drought the zhuoba and the elders must sacrifice three pigs, put the pig's head on the fence of the zhuoba house, and pray for rain while the people jump to take the mud from the pond (Song 2007: 305). They have sacred forests around every village, usually situated more elevated on the slope of the mountain, which provide an ecological shelter to the village against torrential rains, are a reservoir of biodiversity, and play important roles in the spiritual life of the Jino.

The present distribution of Jino villages is believed to have originated by the foremothers establishing each of the main branches of a mother village and a father village. The rest of the villages are believed to be their descendants and situated therefore in a lower ritual position. Jino traditions state that all these villages were established by women. Maybe as a remnant of their former matriarchy the name of many villages contains the meaning of mother or woman. The oldest woman in the village is called A Mo or mother of the whole village (Song 2007: 296; Zhao 1995: 28).

Among the Jino there are three levels of traditional power, family, clan and village power, plus the power of the Dai nobles. The head of the family is called zhuole, and is the eldest male of the family. In the Jino long-house he lived in the first room at right, in front of the spirits room that was on the left, where the souls of the deceased parents were worshipped. He has the right to a share in all animals hunted and to the head of the big game. Before starting the agricultural year he worships the deities and the people work one day in his field before starting working in their own fields. His three main tasks are to lead religious ceremonies, to allocate the land to the members of the family and to arrange the work of each person. (With the disappearance of the long-houses most of the family head represents only his wife and children). The head of the clan is the oldest male of the clan, he has similar functions at clan level. Each village is governed by a council of elders, formed by the leaders of each clan, chaired by the zhuoba, the elder of the clan that arrived first and established the village. In some villages a power structure appointed by the Dai nobles was superimposed, whose main task was to receive taxes and tributes due to the Dai and Chinese administrations (Zheng 2008: 50).

The clan elders are the leaders of the clans, and also of the village. Being the oldest people in the village, they are respected by everybody. They have to serve as village elders as long as they are the oldest people in their clans (Ma 1989). All important matters are decided by the elders. They act as a council of seven elders and seven assistants lead by the zhuoba and the zhuosheng. The zhuoba, the eldest person of the main clan in the village, occupies the highest position. His title means "mother of the village", and the sacred female drum used at all village sacrifices and festivals is stored in his house. Zhuosheng, the oldest male of the second clan, is called the "father of the village" and he keeps the male drum in his house (Yin 2001). The power of the elder's council is democratic, as each man, independently of his character or ability, is entitled to reach this dignity, just if he is healthy enough to become the elder of his clan. Leaders are called by different names in each village, and they are not always seven, but reflect the clan's composition and importance in the village. In Yanuo village there are 4 leaders: zhuoba, dazhai, pubi and laige, which represent the 4 clans of the village.

Zhuoba is the main officiant in the many rituals related with the village deity, which is worshipped by him in the name of the people in many ceremonies. The zhuoba is the "mother of the village" and the village deity a deification of the founding mother. In a way parallel to the rituals in which the emperor in Beijing prayed to his celestial ancestors for the wellbeing of the people, the zhuoba prays his own ancestors to provide wellbeing to the people living in the village. The ancestor can act as the intermediate between the people of the village and the local spirits thanks to the right that she acquired in the mythical time when the village was established. This explains why the village deity must be worshipped in most of the ceremonies, as all relations the people have with local spirits are carried out through the village deity, or sometimes through the soul of the deceased parents (Du 1996: 868). The village deity is the ancestor of the zhuoba. As most of the Jino villages were established by women, this title "mother of the village" assigned to the zhuoba becomes clear when we consider that these ancestral mothers conferred their title and leadership to the elder of their daughters until such time as the men took the title and office.

It seems that in the past each village was composed of two clans, one considered feminine and the other masculine as is suggested by their legends. The mother clan had ritual and political preeminence over the father clan. In this time the zhuoba and the zhuosheng, being the oldest men of the two clans in the village, represented all the villagers. As the Jino rule that marriage must take place inside the village but outside the clan, all villages must have at least two clans. It is possible that the existence of some helpers and a kind of council of elders arose from the need to give voice to the new clans that arrived to live in multi-clan villages. It is interesting to remark that

107

among the Jino and related cultures the number seven is the feminine number: women have seven souls, their pregnancy lasts seven months. The fact that the elder's council has seven members suggests that in the past it was an institution of the matriarchal clan society, when villagers were governed by the seven eldest women leaded by the mother of the village. The fact that the same word that was used to designate the oldest women is now used to name the oldest men seems to confirm this (Du 1991: 409).

The main functions of the Jino elders are related to religious, ritual and ancestral traditions, as the elders embody traditions and are the main defenders of the village. They supervise over religious sacrifices and ceremonies; they represent the villagers in the outside world, mediating in conflicts and caring for the social relations of the villages; manage the resources and organize swiddening. They inspect the borders of the clan and village land, and choose the time of the most important festivals. One of their main duties is to officiate at the ceremony which starts the spring sowing, when they sacrifice an animal and bury some seeds in the soil. Only then can the rest of the villagers start sowing. The New Year is announced by the beating of a big drum and gong in the elders' homes, when all the villagers, young and old, would rush to their homes to sing and dance (Yin 2001: 223).

In carrying out their production activities, the leaders are helped by the rest of the villagers. In the sowing season each family sends a person to help them to sow their fields, and only when they finish, can they start work in their own fields. If they sacrifice an ox, they give them the head as a symbol of respect (Dict: 330).

Besides the two main leaders, the other five elders that form the seven member village council, also have different titles. Koupulou is in charge of financial affairs, Nai'e must slay cattle and serve guests from other villages, Dazai is responsible for communication and mediation, etc (Song 2007: 307).

Jino women hat-shaped houses

The first social researchers in Jino lands found that in the most primitive villages all the patrilineal descendants from one ancestor lived in a longhouse under one roof. We have no data about families living in a longhouse under an old matriarch leadership, but due to the fact that some Lahu neighbors (linguistically and culturally related to the Jino) were reported to live in matriarchal longhouses in the 1950s combined with the matriarchal record of the Jino, the fact that in the past the Jino lived in matriarchal longhouses cannot be disregarded.

The long-houses were rectangular buildings with a front and a back door, wooden beams and supporting wooden posts. Their walls were made of woven bamboo strips and were roofed with thatch secured by vines. There were no windows and lighting during the day was dim. The supporting posts dove-tailed with the main beams and the whole structure was built without nails. Materials for constructing a long-house were readily obtained, its construction was speedy and the result was durable (Zhu 1989). Longhouses were not common to all the Jino, but rather to some villages. Some of them were originally established by the families' tradition of not separating the sons before the death of their parents. In some villages there were families living in long houses and others in small houses (Zheng 2008:11).

Longhouses were very popular in the past, most of the smaller houses found nowadays being a product of the division of longhouses. Until the 1960s, in Yanuo village all the people lived in long-houses: about 500 people altogether. In no other village were there so many long-houses nor were they so large (Zheng 2008: 10). The biggest longhouse was 60 meters long and 10 meters wide. Inside it housed 127 people in 32 rooms divided along both sides of a central corridor with 32 hearths, one for each family. Passing through the door of a long-house one enters into the main hall, whose hearth, built on a square stone platform, was the largest of the entire building. It belonged to the oldest man, who lived in the first room on the right near the front door and it symbolized the patriarchal power and the entire family. Smaller rooms which served as sleeping quarters for each nuclear family ranked in order of seniority. Outside each door was the household hearth, a tripod formed by three upright stones. Other hearths were used for religious purposes or by guests. (Zhu 1989, Zhi 1984: 89, Zhong 1983: 30)

The far right of the guest-room was divided up to form a room for religious purposes. Hanging on the four walls were the skulls and teeth of game killed by the members of the longhouse; a collective display of hunting skill. This room was usually closed to all visitors. When young women reached a certain age, they had to leave the house and marry into a different clan while sons remained there, occupying a new room with their wives (and the children which the wife can take to the wedding). Longhouses continued to grow until it was impossible to enlarge them anymore, at which point new long-houses were built for a family.

The family-head, known as zhuole in some areas, made a unified plan for harvesting. Under his leadership the long-

110

house members worked together, lived together, worshipped together and shared among themselves; a picture of a familial commune under the father's leadership. In bad years when famine prevailed, the family-head would pray for protection before the main hearth. On festive occasions he offered his best wishes to the long-house members and each nuclear family could commence eating only after kowtowing before him (Zhu 1989: 5).

The longhouses now have been replaced by houses of smaller size and the extended families by nuclear ones. Jino villages are big; each one is composed of several dozen houses divided along a main street. Each house is inhabited by a family of between 5 to 8 people that act under the leadership of the father. Houses are built with bamboo, wood and straw, and are supported by five main posts. The one in the middle is the life post. The left one symbolizes the Goddess of the Village and the right one the Goddess of the Hunt. The other two posts are called the parents' post and the goddess' post. The origin of each of these posts is preserved in beautiful legends. While the beams and posts are made of wood, the floor and terraces are made of bamboo, and the roof is made of straw which has been conveniently twisted until it is waterproof (Msd).

Their dualist view of the word is also visible in Jino houses. Each house is built to a north-south axis, facing the sun, with two gates, east for the people, and west for the spirits. Each house also has two terraces, one in the front and another in the back. The front terrace is connected to the stairs, and the back one is for hanging clothes. Houses normally have two stories; the ground floor to store the tools and livestock, and the upper floor serving as the living area for the family. The living quarters are also divided into an outer section and an inner one. The outer section is the main room with the kitchen and

111

hearth, it is the center of family life, where the members of the family eat, work on their handicrafts and discuss family matters. It is also the place to receive the guests. In the inner section there are some rooms for sleeping whose walls are made of bamboo strips.

The hearth is composed of three stones making a tripod; over it is hung a bamboo basket with some food. The hearth and tripod are the most sacred places of the house (Chen Ping 1993: 90). Each of the three stones which formed the hearth's base had a special name and significance. The stone called Kuandou stood for the individual nuclear families of the longhouse. The stone called Zheluo represented the family-head of the longhouse. The stone called Daomi represented the people of the village. The special significance the Jino attach to the stove is likely to reflect three types of land ownership: village ownership, long-house ownership and individual ownership. During the ceremony to eat the new rice the family-head steams rice made from the new grain and carefully studies the direction in which the steam first emanates from the pot, which is believed to point out if the long-house members will enjoy good hunting, if the harvest will be abundant or if a poor crop must be expected (Zhu 1989).

The roof of the houses, whose shape resembles that of the Jino women's hat, sometimes has two sets of earrings as decoration. Common houses have three earrings on each side, while the houses of the zhuoba and other elders have five earrings on each side. These earrings symbolize the spirit of the father and mother in the family. When one of them dies earrings are taken out. Sometime bird's feathers or squirrels' tails can be found hanging near the door; this is a reminder of a tale about two lovers that, being from the same family, and considering the impossibility of getting married, committed suicide in the

112

mountain, changing in two silver pheasants after death (Cheng 1993).

Building a house is an important matter that includes several ceremonies. Jino people build a new house when they feel that their deceased parents are asking them to do so. After some signs, usually interpreted as the will of their parents, they refer to divination to know if they should get a yellow ox, as the sacrifice of the yellow ox signifies the end of the ceremonies which accompany house building (Du 1996).

First they must choose a place to raise the new house, and the head of the family must decide whether the place is auspicious or not. In some villages they simply put some grains of rice in the soil, cover them for one night, and see if the rice changes or not. After a sacrifice by the mopei they go to the mountain to cut a tree for the rafter. After cutting it the mopei, zhuoba and zhuosheng will conduct a ceremony to inform the deceased parents of the family of the raising of the new house. The second day the elders will go to the mountain with the family to select the two main posts of the house. They are very important as when they sacrifice an ox, it will be tied to these posts. After selecting the trees, a chicken is sacrificed to them, smearing its blood on the wood and gluing some feathers to it. The trees will be cut under the watch of the mopei, which expels the evil spirits. As additional protection, a dog would be offered to the spirit of the tree and the spirit of the forest. A myth explains the need to sacrifice a dog as an offering to the spirit of the trees to allow them cut the trees down. The same sacrifice is carried out at the beginning of the "cut tree season" in the fields (Cheng 1993: 94-6).

After letting the three trees dry in the forest they are carried to the village to start the building. Before raising the main post they must kill another dog. In the foundation of this post, a bamboo rat's head, a dog's head, dog's hands and dog's tail must be buried and the post smeared with the blood of a dog. After raising the main post a pig is killed to invite friends and relatives. This post must be raised after sunset in order to avoid the shadow of any person being trapped inside. In the hole of the post taro, ginger and daliu must be buried to ward away evil spirits and as offerings to the spirit of the soil.

Entering the new house is an important ritual. Before it is done, people must invite the spirits of their deceased parents to enter it, symbolically carrying them from the cemetery to the house. Sometimes they build a small straw house near the stairs for their ancestors. Later, before the whole village, the oldest woman of the clan will enter the new house with a torch and a broom. The broom is to wipe away the evil spirits, the torch to light the new hearth. She will wipe the hearth, would arrange the three stones and the iron tripod and will light the hearth for the first time with her torch. After finishing, she instructs the mopei to pray to expel the evil spirits so that the family can enter their new house. Then the head of the family will call the people to enter the house in order of importance: husband, wife, sons and daughters. Each family member must walk three times around the fire. For Jino people three is a number that symbolizes completion. When something is done three times, it means that is complete. Then the head of the family will go to the old house to bring the tools and personal possessions of the family.

The building ceremony ends with the sacrifice of a yellow ox to the spirits of the deceased parents, and a pig and a chicken to other spirits. The sacrifice of the ox is done under the mopei prayers. The youka old lady makes the rope that ties the ox, and a spirits stair to connect the lower section of the post with the upper section, where the parents' tablet hangs. One of the ends of the rope is tied to the ox, the other to the parent's tablet that hangs on the beam. The youka puts a gourd on the ox; the mopei chants a prayer explaining to the deceased parents that this is a sacrifice, asking them to protect the well-being and safety of the family. Then he must shoot three arrows at the ox. If the ox is not killed, it is then killed with a hammer. The head of the ox will be hung on the beam beside the parents' tablet, and the meat offered to different spirits with the pig and chicken meat, eaten by all those present. The mopei receives a leg, some ribs and part of the head of the ox; he will then offer these to the goddess of the mopei to ask for effectiveness in his prayers and he must invite the seven elders of the village to a ritual lunch. The ceremony ends, and the people eat and drink, and happily sing and dance (Cheng 1993). The Wuyou branch, more influenced by Han, do not kill an ox during the house building ceremony, but instead shoot arrows at a pig, and let a hole open in the roof (XSBN 1989: 18).

Most of the Jino families also have a granary near the house. Usually it is not closed, since Jino people do not take anything that belongs to another person. They are not afraid of rats eating their grains and they even sometimes have a kind of wood which lets the rats in. This is because a legend tells that a rat liberated three brothers caught by a demon who intended to eat them (Cheng 1993: 104). Every family also has a simple hut at the edge of the field to rest during the working season (Zhi 1984).

Clothes

The traditional dress of the Jino is simple, elegant and has its own unique characteristics; it varies with the gender, age and ethnic branch to which the wearer belongs (Wei 1992: 225).

Clothes of the three Jino branches show a general pattern with some interesting particularities. Men's jackets are simpler among the Aha branch, with some sun decorations among the Axi, and with more elaborate decorations among the Wuyou, including silver pieces stitched on them. The women's cap is more or less similar among the Aha and the Axi, but with more vivid colors among the Wuyou (XSBN 1989: 34, 49). There are legends that explain the origin of the different clothes for men and women, telling that in the past men and women wore similar clothes, but at night, unable to know if another person was a man or a woman, men sometimes embraced men and women, women. To avoid these embarrassing situations different kinds of clothes were established for men and women (Zheng 2008: 133).

Most Jino women are experts in spinning and weaving. Looms are seen everywhere. They use homemade cloth to make cotton clothes very durable, called "Kandaobu" (cloth which can chop the knife). While spinning, women sit on the ground, with one end of the warp tied to their waists and the other end, tied to two sticks opposite, the wefts winding around the bamboo shuttles. During the operation, they use hands to move the shuttles back and forth, and push the wefts taut with the chopper-shaped board after each round. These cycles continue until one piece is finished. A Jino girl must weave by herself some Kandao cloth as her dowry, and when her father or husband dies, she will hang the cloth on the sacred tree in the graveyard. If the marriage is broken, she merely needs to cut the cloth and this announces her divorce (Song 2007: 302).

Women

The traditional dress of Jino women is simple and elegant. Useful for their daily activities, it constitutes part of a set of symbols that magically connect Jino women with the forces of the universe. In the upper part of their body they wear a short cotton jacket, collarless, that extends to their waist. This jacket is decorated with floral motifs among brightly colored horizontal stripes on the front and an embroidered image of the moon on the back. The stripes represent their ancestors' souls, while the red stripes of the jacket and the hat are symbols of their life strength. Sometimes they also wear a kind of triangle-shaped cloth apron, a symbol of female subjection to male power[1]. They wear long skirts hemmed with a broad red-lace border; and they protect the lower part of their legs from animal biting or possible injuries with leggings that go from the ankle up to just below the knee. Women carry things in baskets on their backs with straps tied around their foreheads (Chinatravel).

The most remarkable feature of Jino women's dress is the hat with which they cover their head. It is a kind of cloth cloak, pointed at the top and reaching the shoulders of the wearer. This hat is made with a piece of cloth, folded in the middle and sewed on one side. The women's hat is seen by the Jino as the model which gives shape to their houses, suggesting a common symbolism in connection with hidden powers and with the protection from danger. As a family is protected under the house roof, so women (maybe as the traditional family chiefs) are protected under their hat, with the same shape.

Women's hats are also a mark of their marital status, as unmarried women's hats are pointed in shape leaving their hair

---

[1] The origin of female aprons is related among some Yunnan minorities to the start of the male domination. They were preceded in many legends by a time in which women were the leaders of the society. After men, usually through a trick, get the leadership, women start to wear aprons, as a piece of cloth, maybe related to be near the hearth, that will prevent them of develop of their potential and regain leadership again (Ceinos 2007).

117

outside, while the hat of married women is flat, with the hair gathered inside it.

The origin of the hat is seen in a Jino legend that tells that long, long ago, a kind old woman put a beautiful jacket on a miserable woman to make her look like a fairy princess. Ever since Jino women have followed this style. Other myths point out that women's clothes were made after the style of their fore-mother who created the heaven and earth (Sun 1996: 111).

Men's clothes

Men's traditional clothes are even simpler. Usually long-sleeved white jackets, without collars or buttons and broad-legged white trousers and a turban. They also show a characteristic decoration that links them with the Jino worldview. In the past, most men kept three strands of hair on the top of their heads. Tradition has it that the one on the forehead was to commemorate Zhuge Liang, while the other two at the sides were to commemorate their parents. In the front part of their jackets they have nine stripes in red, blue and green, representing the nine souls of men (Xing 2008: 77), as well as a number of circular figures embroidered on the back side, which some say show respect and reminiscence for Zhuge Liang, whilst others say that they represent the sun, and correspond with the moon represented in the women's dress (Wei 1992). Even today both Jino men and women go barefoot in the more isolated villages.

Jino women and men have their earlobes pierced, carrying in the earlobe small pieces of wood or metal, or even some flowers. In Jino traditional culture to have ear-holes are considered to be beautiful; they are a symbol of the good qualities in a person. Those who not pierce their ears were

118

considered crazy and were not accepted as belonging to the clan. Usually Jino boys and girls pierced their ear lobes for the first time at the age of seven or eight years old. It was the beginning of a long process of inserting bamboo sticks into the holes and enlarging them by putting thicker ones in from time to time, rendering huge ear-holes apt to be decorated with small bundles of flowers, sometimes changed several times a day. In the past, when the holes reached a certain size, the parents began to teach their children farming and housekeeping. When boys and girls started to stick fresh flowers in the bamboo tubes hanging from their ears, it was a symbol that they have reached maturity for love (Zhong 1983: 27, 29, 89). In the past they painted their teeth black with the sap of the lacquer tree, which besides being a mark of beauty was said to prevent bad breath and tooth decay (Zhi 1984: 90).

Bamboo

Bamboo groves are seen everywhere in the Jino Mountain, and many varieties of bamboo grow there. Jino men excel in weaving bamboo articles. Using thin strips of bamboo they can make excellent handicrafts -different kinds of utensils from cigarette boxes to needle and thread containers. They have in fact created an admirably unique bamboo culture. They always carry with them some bamboo articles or bamboo-plaited pieces of equipment. Bamboo twisting is the men's task, corresponding with the women's weaving.

They build houses with bamboo beams and columns, step on bamboo floors, "sleep in bamboo beds, work with bamboo handled choppers, shovels and hoes, carry loads in bamboo baskets, carry water in bamboo tubes, lead water to the fields in bamboo aqueducts, make tea and cook food in bamboo "pots" and use bowls, chopsticks, spoons and wine and tea mugs, all

119

made of bamboo. Even records are kept on bamboo strips"
(Zhang and Zeng 1993: 236-7). The Jino use bamboo to cook
their food. They drink tea or wine in bamboo cups easily done.
Most of their musical instruments are made of bamboo
including a flute with two finger holes, a vertical flute, a
xiangmie (a local wing instrument), and the *chik*, a xylophone-
like percussion instrument made of seven bamboo pipes of
different lengths and diameters. Bamboo is for them the most
important resource nature provides.

Jino food

Jino food offers the gourmet a range of flavors unknown in
other places. Although their cooking techniques seem simple:
roasting, baking, frying, the fact that they use as condiments a
surprising number of exotic herbs gives each of their dishes a
distinct flavor. Economic development has lead to the opening
of some Jino restaurants in the area, through which their
culinary art is developing. Rice, vegetables and a small amount
of meat constitute their staple foods. Roasted meat is saved for
festivals and ceremonies, when people take the time to enjoy
the slow roasting process.

Chapter 7

Intangible culture of the Jino

The main myths of the Jino are *Amoyaobai* and *Maniu and Mahei*. The first narrates the creation of the world and human beings, and the second the post flood re-creation of humanity. In *Amoyaobai*, the great goddess of the same name, a giantess of inexhaustible force, creates the world and all the animals, plants and human beings that live on the earth. She controlled the relations between human and animals, and ended with the seven suns that scorched the earth, ruling that the rooster must call to the sun every morning. She divided the human beings into Han, Dai and Jino and assigned to each of them their living territories, giving them the main tools and cultural artifacts that nowadays characterize these three peoples. Later she died. She acted both as a creator goddess and as the heroin that brought along civilization, as she taught the Jino the basis of their culture (Ceinos 2007: 93).

Maniu and Mahei or *The origin of making offerings to the ancestors* tells how after the flood only the brothers Mahei and Maniu survived inside a wooden drum. From the gourd's only seed they saved inside the drum, it grew a big gourd tree with a huge gourd that the ancestral couple stored in the roof of their house. Inside this gourd, new humankind was growing; once they were ready to go out they called Mahei and Maniu to open a hole to let them out. But each time they wanted to open the gourd, burning on its surface, somebody stopped them for fear of being burned, until the old woman Apierer asked them to burn in her place, and in this way she sacrificed her life to let the human beings out of the gourd (Ceinos: 2007: 93; Miller 1994).

There are songs and poems that remember the proper way to carry out different tasks, of which the most important is *Puzhuzi,* a guide map to the yearly rituals. Other poems are related to love and marriage customs, emphasizing the proper way to do it, as the famous poem *Bogelei or Love Song,* a romantic poem that describes the love between two young people that knew each other from their childhood, also describing the wedding ceremony and some aspects of it.

There are many folk tales that reflect Jino morals and ethics. For example *Poor Man,* a story about a poor Jino villager that suffers discrimination from the richer families in the village, which don't share their game with him, violating Jino traditional law that states that the product of game must be evenly divided. He is advised by a foreign traveler to leave the village just in time to avoid death by the collapse of a mountain. *Two brothers* tells the story of two brothers that fell in love with the same woman. One is rich and lazy and the other poor and hard-working. All the attempts by the rich brother to gain the favor of the girl are doomed to fail, while the humble gifts that the poor brother gives her are well received. Another tale about brothers is *Men and monkeys,* which tells the history of two brothers that share unevenly their riches. The younger one receives only some gourd seeds from which he sows and grows many gourds. As monkeys usually eat the gourds, he lies over them, feigning death. The monkeys feel very sad for the death of their benefactor, cry bitterly before him and arrange a solemn funeral, in which they put many golden and silver objects near his corpse. Just when the monkeys want to bury him, he awakes and shouts, and the scared monkeys fly away leaving behind all the riches. When the older brother inquires about his sudden fortune he tells him in detail. He follows his brother's instructions but, at the moment when the monkeys place his body on a tree branch waiting to put it in the grave, he shouts and the monkeys fly away scared, loosening the rope, causing the brother to crash down to the earth (Cheng 1993: 117).

In *Girl Fish*, the daughter of the dragon king falls in love with a poor Jino villager. Her father does not allow them to marry due to the poverty of the husband. The Fish Girl then helps her lover to become one of the richest men in the area and they marry. Not long after being married the husband falls in love with another woman. The Fish Girl leaves him and takes all his riches. Seeing him poor again, his new wife also leaves him. He wanders alone the rest of his life mourning his stupid behavior. *Egg Girl* is the story of a celestial woman that descends to the earth to experience human love; she falls in love with a poor Jino boy, but as news of her beauty reach far away, the king comes to take her, and though they try to resist, he kidnaps her. The only way she has to keep in touch with her beloved Jino man is to invite him to ascend heaven together, where he becomes the sun and she the moon, and they meet only once every three years, the time at which people see an eclipse of the moon.

Basi and Misi is a tragic love story in which two young lovers living in different villages fall in love during the New Year festival. The forced separation that came after the festivities ended fills the two lovers with sorrow. The certainty that their love will have no future, since people must marry in the same village, slowly consumes their hopes of a hypothetical marriage. Misi is married with a husband she dislikes, and Basi assures her that if they had no chance to live together at least they will have the chance to be together at death. This poem is a perfect complement to the history of the goddess of the hunt. Both marriages were doomed to failure, one because the lovers were too near and the other because they were too far. The last recourse to suicide by the lovers in both poems point out that here also, as among the Lahu, the Naxi and other ethnic groups in Yunnan, suicide was one of the options young people had to put an end to their problems in love.

Atui is the Jino trickster, a clever persona always striving to help the poor and mock the rich. His stories are loved by the people. Though in some anthologies he is shown as constantly mocking the rich, his humor is more natural, lacking the class conscience that did not exist in an egalitarian society.

Music

Music constitutes a fundamental part of Jino lives. Their myths and legends are usually conveyed through songs, and weddings and funerals are performed under the rhythm of music. Love and labor, hunting and feasting, all the daily activities of the Jino are accompanied by corresponding songs. In Jino villages there are often one or two old women who are masters of traditional songs. Among their traditional songs, the most common are *Basi* or love songs, *Zi*, a type of folk song about customs concerning production, life and sacrificial rites, and the sacred songs chanted by the bailapao and mopei to control the spirits (Zhao 1995: 22; Song 2007: 296).

The Jino use many musical instruments. While some of them are imported from Dai or Han areas, the two most alluring, the *chik* and the drum, are their own creation. The chik or qike is a percussion instrument made of seven bamboo tubes of different sizes that produce seven different pitches. At the bottom of each bamboo tube is a knot, and the top is slanted with a vertical slot on the lower edge; the pitch of the sound is determined by the length of the bamboo, its diameter, and the length of the slot. The *chik* was first used by hunters to convey messages when they captured wild animals. Their origin, according to the legends, lies in the custom of Jino hunters of cutting some bamboo tubes of different sizes and beating them on the way back home after a hunting expedition. Listening to their music people in the village could tell if the shoot was abundant and which animals they will bring. Later, the bamboo tubes were refined and developed by some folk artists into today's seven-scaled instrument that sounds pleasant and melodious and was also played in music festivals and at joyful celebrations. The *bugu* has the same structure and shape as the chik, but it is bigger, and is used only after getting a big animal on the way back to the village. In the past, only men could beat the tubes, since they were associated with hunting (Zhao 1995: 25; Du and Yip 1993: 224; Cheng 1993: 134).

The wooden drum is the most sacred of Jino sacrificial implements, as it represents the embodiment of the Deity of the Village that protects the village and is also a transformation of the body of the elders. It is about 1.5 meters from face to face and 80 cm in diameter, covered with cowhide on both sides. It is placed across a stand about the height of one person. Usually stored in the zhuoba's home, it is highly respected and it cannot be beaten or moved at will, but only at the Temaoke Festival and other religious ceremonies.

Making the wooden drum is an extremely important activity for every village and has a strict set of procedures, with a lot of potential taboos. They must go to the mountain to select one tree, then choosing an auspicious day to sacrifice a chicken before the tree and cutting it. Women and children cannot see the drum before it is finished and the sunrays must not reach the trunk, so it is covered with straw. The men that cut, carve and arrange the cover of the big drum must work at night, without letting the sunrays touch the drum, as they are afraid the shadows of the people could fall inside the drum. Before closing the drum they put some offerings inside and the zhuoba sacrifices a chicken to the drum, praying for the sound "to welcome the spirit of silver and grain, to call the nine souls of the men and the seven souls of the women." That is, praying to bring riches and children. After closing the drum they make offerings to the animals that hang from its nails.

When the covering is finished, the sacrifice ceremony is repeated again, and people dance around the Drum Dance happily. After that, people carry the wooden drum to zhuoba or zhuosheng's house to be consecrated, singing and dancing all the way. The drum, as a symbol of the village god, can only be beaten on three occasions: at the Temaoke festival, when worshipping the god of the family and when they made a new house for the zhuoba. (Zhu 2009: 75).

Other musical instruments commonly used among the Jino are wind instruments such as the xiao vertical flute (*bietuo*), the flute of stalks of rice (*biebie*), the suona (*biela*), the whistle (*biebei*), and two kinds of local bamboo flutes known as *biechulu* and *bieshi*. Their main string instrument is a kind of guitar with three strings called sanxiang among the Chinese and *dite* in their language. They occasionally use tree leaves (*abo* in their language), mouth's harp, etc.

Dance

126

Their main and most representative dance is Ezhiguo or the Dance of the Big Drum, a ritual dance by means of which the Jino express their respect to their goddesses and ancestors, which have different names and characteristics from one place to other. It is danced in the New Year, at the time of rising of a new house and at ceremonies for deceased parents. At New Year the drum is beaten and the people dance around it to thank Amoyaobai for sending their ancestors into the world.

When they dance around the drum they have three main steps, one is a kind of prayer to show their respect to the spirit of the drum, the second is a happy dance and the third is a celebratory dance. During the dance people form a circle around the drum. Two drummers first pay respect to the crowd and then to the drum, and lead the crowd in the performance of these three movements. In the past, the drum was only beaten by the zhuoba leaders, with the accompanying sound of gongs and cymbals. Later, girls also beat the drum while boys dance around. "Before 1949 women could beat only the back of the drum and dance behind rather than in front of it. The strict set of procedures and rules they had to follow when dancing the Great Drum Dance added a touch of mystery to the dance" (Cheng 1993: 134; Li 1987: 62- 65).

"The dancers first stand there with both feet on the ground naturally and both hands clasping drumsticks, and then the left foot sets forward and touches down the ground, the left knee bends and both legs shake. After that, the left hand holds a drumstick and raises it overhead and the right hand grasps a drumstick keeping it at the right hip. Then the left hand puts down and the right hand rises up. After the movement of turning around, the dancer exchanges the posture of the left and right foot" (New).

127

Now the Jino drums are called sun-drums because on each of their sides they have about ten sticks inserted to resemble a sun with its sunrays. There is a complete set of ritual before the big drum dance: before the dance the elders offer a pig and a chicken before the drum, whilst one of them recites the sacrificial words. Praying to the big drum can bring peace and prosperity to them. After the sacrifice, one person holds drumsticks in his two hands while dancing, and others dance playing cymbals. The singing words of big drum are called *wuyouke*, and are related to the history, morality and customs of the Jino (New).

In the past they had a rich catalogue of ritual and love dances, whose movements were related to the activity done, sach as Shaguoke, the dance of the new house, or Tuojika, the dance of pestle the grain, performed after the death of old people. Below the stairs of the deceased's house; a dancer holds a big pestle and rhythmically pestles the rice among two or four people that hold the rice (XSBN 1989: 45, 59).

Among their funerary dances they have Dakeguo or the dance of the bamboo pole, danced only by men before the house of a deceased person. Three men seated in a triangle hold three sticks of bamboo over which the dancer would jump repeatedly. Zheke zhui or the dance around the bamboo pole, is a dance to worship the ancestors. Two bamboo poles are nailed to the ground, on the top of which are put some flowers, and between them three horizontal poles. The dancers move around this structure. Siqiu or peaceful funeral is performed in Buyuan area, at night, inside the house of the deceased. Men and women hold hands and form a circle, singing and dancing slowly. Amo Songtie ji is performed every night after the death of one of the seven elders of the village

128

until the corpse is buried. Later they go with the family to the cemetery, still dressed in women´s dancing clothes and masks occasionally, but without dancing, and dance again when the family returns to the village (XSBN 1989: 56 - 72).

Childdren's dances are danced in happy situations or just casually. From 5 to 12 years old Jinuo children are enrolled in a kind of educative village institution called *ruozainike*, where their main task is to sing, dance and play. Zhuguneng or Girls' Dance is performed by girls from 13 years old to the moment they marry. Under the light of the moon the girls meet in the village square every night to sing and dance. They form a circle with their arms placed across one another's shoulders, leaning forward, in simple and elegant movements singing happy songs and love songs, the rhythm of which varies considerably with each performance (XSBN 1989: 106, Li 1987: 62-5).

Epilogue

Present life of the Jino

Jino traditional culture as described in this book does not exist anymore; it is now a matter of the past. Economical, political and social transformations of the last 50 years have shattered the Jino traditional worldview, substituting it for an ethnic vision of the global world whose features are as yet undefined.

Customs, beliefs, traditions, geography, economy: all were closely integrated with traditional Jino society, and each of these aspects of their existence can be understood only with reference to their psychological framework surrounding their relationship with the original goddess through their legendary genealogy of mothers, the protection covered by the goddesses that govern each of their daily activities, and the duty to take care of mother earth and its resources in a sustainable way.

After the first socialist reforms of 1958 and the upset during the years of the Cultural Revolution, in the late 1970s Jino society again suffered political reforms which originated far from their lands. They were gradually encouraged to enter local and regional markets to satisfy their economic needs. Communal land was transferred to households. Government policies encouraged the Jino people to develop paddy fields as a replacement for swidden agriculture. Working these paddy rice fields radically transformed their living patterns. In a few years most of the Jino villages moved, high-altitude sites were rejected in favor of low altitude ones, mountain settlements in favor of valleys, and the isolation in remote retreats where they feel safe from possible enemies was exchanged in favor of the highway neighborhood that made their access to the market and the outer world easy (Fu 2005: 367).

Reform in the forestry sector began in 1981, when the government took the control of forest tenure and production, with no regard for Jino's traditional knowledge of their forest. Constant changes in forest management policies hindered the efforts to preserve biodiversity and to develop forestry. Trees were removed as timber for both local needs and for sale. Entire tracts of forest were converted into rubber and tea plantations to adapt to the increasing market demand, destroying some forest ecosystems. On the other hand dry lands not fit for cultivation were reverted back to forest, their protection encouraged by converting them to nature reserves (Fu 2005; Lu and Kang 2006). Market demands for non-timber forest products increased, greatly driven by expanding tourism and the economic development of Chinese society. This brought considerable cash income to many Jino families (Wang).

All these changes, happily received by the Jino, have also had potentially adverse effects. Rubber development as an alternative to fallow agriculture has weakened food security seriously. The diversity of upland rice varieties used in fallow agriculture is quickly disappearing. As Jino households, with more cash income, do not need to worry about fulfilling their food needs (as they can buy rice from the market) they cultivate fewer upland rice varieties and concentrate instead on the select varieties with good quality and better yields. The hill farmers with their hundreds of rice varieties, their many intercropped vegetables and fruits, and their cyclical farming methods are gradually disappearing (Fu 2005).

131

Traditional indigenous varieties of rice, closely linked with the customs and farming methods of the Jino, are threatened not only by the introduction of exotic varieties with high yield and wild ecological tolerances but also by the loss of fallow fields, meaning that many traditional varieties are no longer in cultivation. Lack of fallow fields lead to the loss of maize plantations and several historically cultivated maize varieties may be lost. Household cultivated traditional paddy rice varieties had dropped from 36.7% in 2000 to 0 in 2003. Similarly, household cultivated traditional upland rice varieties had dropped from 86.7% in 2000 to 3.3% in 2003. Furthermore, the number of cultivated rice varieties has gradually declined. The loss of species and varieties is mirrored in the loss of traditional cultivation techniques. Traditional knowledge of land classification, the basis of fallow agriculture, is being lost as hybridized varieties that can adapt to different environments are planted widely (Fu 2005: 369).

Leaving the isolation of their mountains to enter the modern world has caused considerable psychological strain to the Jino. Considering their traditional culture as the main cause of their backwardness, Jino students regard school as the only way to escape poverty (Hanse 1999: 144). It is here that they give up their culture and language to learn both oral and written Chinese (Zhao 1995: 15), knowing that learning Chinese is the gate to success. On the other hand everyday contact with the outer world, and the familiarity with outside cultures, provides Jino students with a new vision of themselves and their culture, and if most of the aspects of their traditional religion are rejected as superstitions a new cultural construction is growing in its place, one in which educated Jino members may challenge their own peripheral and subordinate position within the local ethnic hierarchy (Hanse 1999: 156).

Due to the impact of mainstream Chinese lifestyle and culture, the Jino's traditional ideals, customs, lifestyle, ethics and morality and language have been challenged in the process of modernization. Their traditional society has lost its social structure, belief system and rituals, which in turn forces the people to face the stress of adjustment and the risk of losing self and ethnic identity (Leff, 1981). Jino people face acculturation and assimilation tendencies which are creating difficulties for each individual, producing in some instances serious mental health problems, as well as higher rates of crime, suicide, divorce, alcohol and other drug abuse. Crimes for economic reasons have increased significantly. Pathological drinking and alcoholism have become a prominent public problem, and alcohol abuse has become one of the main reasons for family dispute, public security problems, crimes and suicide. Many young Jino women have left the Jino mountain area for more job opportunities, some of them engaging in sex trade, which produces and increases the problem of male bachelordom for the Jino people (Li et al 2008: 4).

In 1979, due to the poor traffic conditions and their own traditional beliefs, Jino people sought health advice mainly from their traditional healers, which treated diseases with herbs and spiritual rituals. With the development of modern living conditions and the improvement of communications most of them now prefer modern medicine treatments for different kind of diseases, especially for physical diseases, though some of them still resort to witch doctors and herbs medicine for mental disorders (Li et al 2008: 7).

Nowadays, while each individual Jino enjoys a better life in a more comfortable environment, the unique culture that in the past allowed them to survive for centuries in their difficult environment is quickly disappearing. In the middle of a process of vertiginous changes in the local, national and global arena it is impossible to venture how the Jino culture of the future will be, which of their wonderful cultural creations, the reason for which they were created having now disappeared, will be doomed to oblivion and which of them will remain as an ethnic marker of Jino culture for future generations.

However the study of Jino culture shows to the interested reader two cultural instances which may be unique among the peoples of our world. First is a more or less mythical, legendary account of the first steps of their society as a matriarchal one and its transformation to a patriarchal one, as well as the multitude of instances in which this transformation has not yet happened, leaving matriarchal remnants in most of the Jino cultural characteristics. The second is to show how an efficient use of fallow agriculture can be the best tool to protect the forest and the environment. As this issue is vital even today for the political consideration of the national elites of some countries of Southeast Asia, and therefore to the survival of some of their forest populations, we consider that the Jino provide a good example of how fallow agriculture and forest preservation may be perfectly combined in a sustainable way.

Annex

Amoyaobai created the world: Jino foundation myth

1. In olden times the universe was a vast ocean completely void of substance. Amoyaobai was the first being that appeared in the world. She was a giant of inexhaustible strength that needed to eat 500 kilograms of food every day. She can do many things and can do them quickly; she can pick up two mountains at the same time. Hovering in the air she discovered that the earth was an immense barren sea, without a place to rest her feet. Then with her two hands she raised the earth and the vast sea was transformed into a plain of land. To check if the land was firm or not she pressed with her fingers in different places. The places where she pressed became the concavities of the earth, the places she did not press became the convexities, and in this way the surface of the earth revealed plain lands, deep valleys and high mountains.

She then flew again in the sky and saw the gray and yellow surface of the earth, without any life, with an oppressing dead air everywhere, all barren land. Amoyaobai then rubbed her hands and she used this filth to make pigs, horses, cows, sheep, deer, squirrels and fish: the animals that live on land and in water. She then took a piece of meat from each animal to mould an elephant (this is the reason elephants are bigger than other animals). In this way animals appeared on the earth's surface. There were however many rats, which everywhere stole things to eat. Amoyaobai created the cats to control the rats.

The animals having been created they had nothing to eat. Amoyaobai scratched her head and taking with her fingers the roots of some hairs she created vegetables. Animals then had something to eat.

Amoyaobai then created the human beings, but humans were mixed with the other animals and they were bullied by the animals: when the adults went out to work children were eaten by elephants; wasps with big heads in big groups were found everywhere and in one day they could completely eat the entire body of a small child, leaving only bones. In the river there were some lizards that could suck the blood of the people. The people complained to Amoyaobai: "Big goddess Amoyaobai. You are our ancestor, we were created by you. First there was you and later we were created. Now, our descendants are killed by elephants, big headed wasps and river lizards that eat them. What can we do?"

After hearing their complains Amoyaobai instructed the people to make some oil presses and to use them to control the elephants. Then, when the elephants came to eat the children the people ask the elephants to enter by way of these oil presses, telling them that in this place there was plenty of a lot of tasty oil. However when the elephants were in the middle of the presses men closed them with all their strength and the elephants cried with pain: "Quick, let us go, quick let us go." But the people told them: "If you agree that in the future you will not eat our babies anymore we will set you free; if you don't agree, we will close it until you are dead." The elephants only could agree, and from then on elephants do not eaten babies.

Regarding the problem of the wasps with big heads, Amoyaobai divided the year into four seasons. Spring, summer, autumn, and winter. When winter arrived, and heavy snow fell everywhere the big headed wasps froze to death. Amoyaobai then taught the people to make some tools by twisting bamboo, and how to put these tools in the water in such a way that when the water passed through them it sounded "kala kala". When the water lizards heard it they were scared and did not dare to come near the people and suck their blood.

Now human beings were happy but the animals were not, and they also complained to Amoyaobai. Some animals said that they were killed in a cruel way, and that humans eat them too much. Turtledove said that the people shoot her with their crossbows, piercing her chest. Wild boar and bear complained that people came with firelocks and crossbows to kill them and that they even pursue them. Fish said that human beings used nets to catch them and they were caught inside the nets without any chance of piercing the nets and escaping. Animals in disorder asked Amoyaobai to send thunder and kill the human beings. Amoyaobai listed to them without saying a word.

However not all the animals wanted to annihilate the human beings. At this moment the swallow said: "All of what you have said is untrue. Humans are not unfairly treating animals. Take myself for instance. I live under man's roof for the winter. The people below make fire and sleep and I sleep in my nest very warm. People don't beat me; they don't kill me, nor bully me. Turtledove, you have your wings, when people go to hunt you with their crossbows, why don't you fly away? Fish, why don't you think of a way to escape from the people nets?

Wild boar, bear, are you not eating man's crops? How can the people not injure you? When it finished speaking the swallow came back to the people's house.

All the animals were very excited, each of them told of their own experiences, each of them different, until the moment when they started to separate. Amoyaobai though that the words of the swallow were reasonable, but she also saw that humans walked too quickly, in a way that it was too easy for them to catch the animals and the birds. If she did not change something it was possible that in the future some animals could be hunted to extinction. So she thought that it would be better to make men walk slower. Originally the people legs were straight, without knees, and they ran very quickly. Amoyaobai then put knees in the legs of the people, forcing them to walk slower and avoid killing too many animals. Amoyaobai did not send the thunder to kill the people; she is extremely kind to the people.

2. After many, many years seven suns suddenly appeared in the sky. Their scorching heat made life of any being impossible. The soil was burnt, iron knives and trees were burnt by the suns, big trees thousands of years old suddenly withered, mottled ox and pigs were also scorched to death. Human beings had no way of keeping alive. People then rose to shoot the suns. The seven suns, frightened, remained on one side of heaven, thinking it would be better to remain hidden.

Without sun the world changed, it was plunged into complete darkness. If a person extended his arms he could not see his fingers. In the middle of the darkness the people could not live, animals could not live. Human beings had no other solution than to go ask the suns: "Sun, please rise again to light the world, without your brightness we cannot sow our crops, we cannot hunt wild animals. We cannot live!" But the suns did not agree to come out, they remained hidden for a long time at the border of heaven. The people arranged a lot of wine, vegetables, and rice and went to ask the deity of heaven to order the sun to rise again to light up the world. But the suns still did not rise.

In the end the human beings went to ask Amoyaobai. The goddess told them to wrap a headless chicken and to put it on the top of a stick, teaching it to call "ji, ji" and the sun will rise. People followed her instructions and when the chicken called, from the edge of heaven one sun suddenly rose. The world slightly lit up, and the people could work happily again. Later, when the people raise new houses and kill oxen they must put in the back of the ox a killed chicken with its head hidden under its wings, in a way that it appears as if a headless chicken. This chicken is a sacrifice to the sun deity.

3. After creating the world, Amoyaobai divided human beings into Han, Dai and Jino nationalities. She then called the people from these three nationalities to divide the world between them. But the Jino, living far away, did not arrive on time. Everybody waited for them for seven days and seven nights, but they still did not appear. Amoyaobai herself went to invite them, but the Jino were very timid, and it remained the same however many times they were called, they did not dare to come. Amoyaobai got angry and turning her head she went back. When she arrived at Kongming Mountain (Sijiezhuomi) her heart softened and she thought that if the Jino people did not attend the division of the world later then their lives would be very hard. Then in this mountain she took some tea seeds, sowing them after her near Manka and Longba villages. From then on the production of tea in these two villages is very good.

After dividing the world Amoyaobai called again the Han, Dai and Jino nationalities to divide the working tools. The Han got the horse headstall and later they rode horses to do their business. The Dai got a bamboo pole to carry things, so they live in the plains and use their poles to carry grain. The honest Jino people got a basket to carry things on their backs, so even today they carry things on their backs in the mountains.

After arranging the way of life of the people Amoyaobai determined that among the men the most elevated must be Asezimo or the head of the village, and the place where the people from every direction will gather must be in the house of the Asezimo, and the time when people from every direction will gather in Asezimo's house will be during the festivals.

From the day she divided the tools Amoyaobai determined that the family of the mouse of the glutinous rice will live in caves in the mountain, the family of the rat in dens made below the earth, the family of the squirrels will spend their days in the trees. She also decided that deer, wild boars, tigers and hedgehogs will live high in the mountains; birds will live inside the forests of the mountains feeding on the trees' fruits and insects. The family of the fishes will live in the water, and they will lay eggs to reproduce in the season when a hundred flowers blossom.

4. After dividing all these things carefully, Amoyaobai called the Han and asked them to give a written language to the Jino. The Han wrote their characters in a cow skin which they handed to the Jino. The Jino took this skin, but when they were crossing a river on their way back home, the characters in the skin were washed away by the water. Seeing this disaster the Jino put the skin to dry out in the fire, trying to save some

characters, but they roasted and roasted, and in the end the skin was burnt, and it was impossible to see any characters. The Jino, suddenly inspired, though that maybe if they eat the characters, they will be able to remember them later. So they ate them. But after eating them they still could not remember a single character. In this way, the Jino people lost their writing.

5. After giving the people their quiet lives Amoyaobai went to the bank of the Mekong River to make some fields, building fields from the north to the south. All the rice fields outside the Jino Mountains were created by her. One day, when she carried two mountains to make fields in the Jino Mountains, some people who hated her made some holes in her pole, putting some knives inside the holes. When Amoyaobai arrived in the western part of Jino Mountain, in the area around Xiao Mengyang, her pole broke and the two mountains fell into Xiao Mengyang. Now the Jino call these mountains "Eji", whose meaning is "Mountains created by Amoyaobai". The broken pole flew into the Mekong River, making a bay in the river in the shape of a bow. The knives hidden inside it hurt her shoulders, from which a fountain of blood surged.

After suffering this injury Amoyaobai called again each of the different tribes, giving them their last instructions. The Jino arrived late again. On the third day they were still hurrying to arrive, and the instructions to the other tribes had already been given. Amoyaobai, with her last breath, told the Jino the name of each kind of animal and plant and taught them the way to use purple glue to secure the knife handle - put purple glue on the knife handle, burn the knife in the fire until red-hot, then put in the handle, which will thus be glued vsecurely. After saying these words, Amoyaobai died.

After her death the Jino mourned her for 13 days. Nowadays "The Worship Dragon Festival" has descended from this time. On the day to worship the dragon nobody can go outside, and it is forbidden to sing or dance inside the village, speak in a loud voice or laugh. Outside people are not allowed to enter the village, and he who violates these rules thus shows that he has no respect for the ancestor Amoyaobai, and he is violating Jino etiquette.

Bibliography

Bai Zhihong and Zhang Xiaoping. *The Dai and the Jinuo people in Xishuangbanna*. In Gan Xuechun. The Yunnan ethnic groups and their cultures. Yunnan Peoples Press. Kunming. 2000.

Brenzinge, Matthias. *Language diversity endangered*. 2007.

Cahill. Susanne E. *Transcendence and Divine Passion: The Queen Mother of the West in Medieval China*. Stanford University Press. 1993.

Ceinos Arcones, Pedro. *Matriarcado en China: madres, reinas, diosas y chamanes*. Miraguano. Madrid. 2011.

Ceinos Arcones, Pedro. *Leyendas de la Diosa Madre (y otros mitos de diosas y mujeres de los pueblos de China)*. Miraguano. Madrid. 2007.

Ceinos Arcones. Pedro. *Sons of Heaven, Brothers of Nature. The Naxi of Southwest China*. Papers of the White Dragon. Kunming. 2012.

Chinatravel. *Jinuo Ethnic Minority*. www.chinatravel.com-/facts/chinese-culture-and-history/chinese-ethnic-groups/jinuo-ethnic-minority/. Accessed 20120423

Cheng Ping. Jinuo fengsu (*Jino Folklore*). Central Institute of the Nationalities. Beijing. 1993.

Committee for the Compilation of Old Documents of the Nationalities of Yunnan. Basi yu Misi - Jino zu minjian changsi (*Basi and Misi - A long folk poem of the Jino Nationality*). Yunnan Nationalities Press. Kunming. 1996.

Deng Qiyao and Zhang Liu. *The Festivals in the Mysterious land of Yunnan*. Yunnan Peoples Publishing House. Kunming, 1991.

Dictionary of the folklore of Chinese national minorities (Zhongguo shaoshu minzu minsu dacidian). Inner Mongolian People Press. Hothot. 1994.

Du Roufu and Yip, Vincent F. *Ethnic Groups in China.* Science Press. Beijing. 1993.

Du Shanshan. *Chopsticks only work in pairs: gender unity and gender equality among the Lahu of southwest China.* Columbia University Press. New York. 2002.

Du Yuting. Jinuo zu (*The Jino Nationality*). Nationalities Press. Beijing. 1989

Du Yuting. Jinuozu juan. In Zhongguo ge minzu yuanshi zongjiao jicheng ziliao. Yizu juan, Baizu juan, Naxi zu juan (*Volume of the Jino Nationality in collected materials about the original religions of each nationality in China, volume of the Yi, Bai and Jino nationalities*). China Academy of Social Sciences. Beijing, 1996.

Du Yuting. *Etnia Jino.* In Yan Ruxian. Matrimonio y familia de las etnias minoritarias de China. Foreign Languages Press. Beijing. 1991.

Du Yuting. *The cultural Constructions of Love in Jinuo Tradition.* Yunnan Peoples Press. Kunming. 2008

E56. *The Jinuo (Jino) Nationality.* www.e56.com.cn/system_file/minority/e-mu/jinuo-e.htm. Accessed 20120425

Eorc (*Encyclopedia of the Original Religions of China*). Zhonguo Yuanshi zongjiao baike quanshu. Chengdu. 2003.

Fu Yongneng, Guo Huijun, Chen Aiguo, Cui Jingyun. *Rubber development by smallholder farmers in Xishuangbanna, Yunnan, China, a case study from Daka and Baka.* 2006.

Fu Yongneng, Guo Huijun, Chen Aiguo, and Cui Jinyun. *Fallow Agroecosystem Dynamics and Socioeconomic Development in China: Two Case Studies in Xishuangbanna Prefecture, Yunnan Province.* Mountain Research and Development Vol 25 No 4 Nov 2005: 365–371.

Grand. Zhongguo ge minzu zongjiao yu shenhua dacidian (*Grand Dictionary of Religion and Myths of Chinese Minorities*). Xueyuan Publishers. Beijing. 1990.

Giersch, Charles Patterson. *Asian Borderlands: the Transformation of Qing China's Yunnan Frontier.* Harvard University Press. 2006.

Groot, JJM. *The religious system of China.* Brill. 1892.

Hanse, Mette Halskov. *Lessons in being Chinese: minority education and ethnic identity in southwest China.* University of Washington Press. 1999.

Harvey Neo and Li-Hui Chen. *Household income diversification and the production of local meat: the prospect of small-scale pig farming in Southern Yunnan,* China. Area. 2008.

Norihiko Hayashi. *The Historical Development of Youle Jino.* Senri Ethnological Studies 75: 255–280_c. 2009.

He Yuanzhi et all. *The traditional Chinese Festivals and Tales.* Chongqing Publishing House. 2005.

Li Jinyin. *Jinuo Dances.* In Chen Weiye, Ji Lanwei and Ma Wei. Flying Dragon and Dancing Phoenix – An Introduction to selected Chinese Minority Folk Dances. New World Press. Beijing. 1987.

Li Jianhua et all. *Twenty-two years longitudinal follow-up study on the mental health status of the Jino nationality in Yunnan province of China.* WCPRR Jan 2008: 4-7

Long Chunlin and Zhou Yilan. *Indigenous community forest management of Jinuo people's swidden agroecosystems in southwest China.* Biodiversity and Conservation. Volume 10, Number 5, 753-767. 2001.

Long Chunlin et all. *Biodiversity Management and Utilization in the Context of Traditional Culture of Jinuo Society in S Yunnan, China.* Acta Botanica Yunnanica. 1999, 21(2):239-248

Lu Xing and Kang Xiaofeng. *Basic Information of Jinuo Minority and Baya Village, Jinuo Township, Jinghong County.* MLI workshop on Conflict Management. Jinghong, China, 2006.

MSD. The Jinuo Ethnic group. www.**msd**china.org/userfiles-/file/pdf/Jino.pdf. Access 24-10-2012.

Ma Changyi. *Zhongguo shenhua gushi* (Tales from Chinese myths). China Tv Press. 1996.

Ma Yin. *China's Minority Nationalities*. Foreign Languages Press. Beijing. 1989.

Mathieu, Christine. *A History and Anthropological Study of the Ancient Kingdoms of the Sino-Tibetan Borderland – Naxi and Mosuo*. Mellen Press. 2003

Miller, Lucien. *South of the Clouds: Tales of Yunnan*. University of Washington Press. 1994.

Matisoff, James A. *Handbook of Proto-Tibeto-Burman: System and Philosophy of Sino-Tibetan Reconstruction*. University of California Press. 2003.

Nelson, Sarah M. *Shamanism and the Origins of States*: Spirit, Power, and Gender in *East Asia*. Left Coast Press. 2008.

New. *Jinuo Nationality "Big Drum Dance"*. hwww.newchina-tour.com/traditions/Folk_Art/395.html. Access 21-3-2012.

Outlook of the culture of the Jino Nationality (Jinuo zu wenhua daguan). Yunnan Nationalities Press. 1999

Ramsey, S. Robert. *The Languages of China*. Princeton University Press. 1987

Song Liying. *Indigenous Ethnic Groups in Yunnan*. Yunnan University Press. Kunming. 2007.

Sun Wei. *Selected photographs of traditional games of China's 56 nationalities*. Kunming. 1996.

Sun Wei. *Oriental Rosy Clouds: Traditional costumes of the 56 Nationalities in China*. Kunming. 1996.

Wang Jieru. *Social change in the economic transformation of livelihoods: Voices from the upland Mountain Community in Southwestern China*. RCSD. Chiangmai. 2004.

Wang Jieru. *Changing Hidden Ethnic Relationship under Non-Timber Forest Products Flow in Transition to Market Economy: Case from Jinuo Community, Southern Yunnan Province, China.* http://dlc.dlib.indiana.edu/dlc/bitstream/handle/10535/423/Wang_Jieru.pdf?sequence=1 Accessed 20120201.

Wang Jieru, Long Chunlin. *Ethnobotanical study of Traditional edible plants of Jinuo Nationality.* Acta Botanica Yunnanica [1995, 17(2):161-168]

Wei Ronghui. *The Chinese National culture of Costume and Adornment.* China Textile Press. 1992.

West, Barbara A. *Encyclopedia of the peoples of Asia and Oceania, Volumen 1.* 2009

Xing Li. *China's Minority Costumes.* China Intercontinental Press. 2008.

XSBN. Xishuangbanna Office of Culture. Jinuo zu minjian wudao (*Popular dances of the Jinuo nationality*). Kunming. 1989.

Xu Yixi. *Headdresses of Chinese minority Nationality women.* Beijing. 1989.

Ye Dabing. *The Bridal Boat. Marriage Customs of China Fifty Five Ethnic Minorities.* New World Press. 1993.

Yin Shaoting. *People and Forest – Yunnan Swidden Agriculture in Human-Ecological Perspective.* Yunnan Education Publishing House. Kunming, 2001.

Yin Shaoting. *Work reports on the project for the construction of ethnic cultural and ecological villages in Yunnan Province, China.* Yunnan Nationalities Press. Kunming. 2002.

Yu Xiqian. Jinuo zu wenhua lun (*Discussions about the Jinuo culture*). Yunnan Nationalities Press. Kunming. 2000

Yunnan. *Jinuo Ethnic minority.* http://www.yunnanadventure.com/article-g465-jinuo-ethnic-minority. Accessed 12-11-2012.

Zhang Weiwen and Zeng Qingnan. *In Search of China's Minorities.* New World Press. Beijing. 1993. p. 235-241.

Zhang Yun- *The Jino minority of China* (Zhongguo Jinuo zu). Ningxia Peoples Press. 2012.

Zhao Jie. *The restless female souls- The Jinuos*. Yunnan Education Publishing House. Kunming. 1995.

Zheng Shaoyun. *The Last Long House: The patrilineal Family and cultural transformation of the Jinuo People*. Yunnan Peoples Press. Kunming. 2008.

Zhi Exiang. *The Jinuos: China's newest Nationality*. In China Reconstructs. China' Minority Nationalities. Beijing. 1984. Pp. 86-93.

Zhong Xiu. *Yunnan Travelogue- 100 days in Southwest China*. New World Press. Beijing. 1983.

Zhu Baotian. *A preliminary account of Jinuo Long-houses*. Thai-Yunnan newsletter 6-1989.

Zhu Yangzhan. *The Temaoke festival of the Jinuo people*. Yunnan Peoples Press. Kunming. 2009.

Glossary

Bailapao: The main ritual specialist. He is in charge of the religious rituals and sacrificial activities, and he usually can divine.

Bugu: A musical instrument with the same structure and shape than the chik, but of a bigger size. It is used only after get a big animal on the way back to the village.

Chik or qike. A percussion instrument made of seven bamboo tubes of different sizes that produce seven different pitches. Usually played when going back home after a hunting expedition.

Daliu. A bamboo net used as talisman that protects houses and villages against the evil spirits. The many holes that remain between the interlaced bamboos make crazy the spirits that feel unable to count them.

Laogan relations: a kind of brotherhood established between Jino and Dai individuals living in neighbor communities.

Mikao. Young associations in which the Jino girls enroll after the passing of age ceremony. This association allow them to gradually become familiar with their adult responsabilities.

Mopei. The shaman of the Jino. He is in charge of important rituals as he can face directly the evil spirits. He is in charge of expelling evil spirits.

Neique People that can release the spirits. It is supposed that he can put spirits in a place and harm other person, making him fell sick or even die.

Polei. A kind of exclusive youth club to which only selected young belong, which help the adults in different celebrations.

Raokao. Youth clubs. After the passing of age ceremony young boys must live inside a raokao, where under the direction of older youths they will learn his role in Jino society.

Wurere: Rite of passage of the Jino.

Youka. Is the oldest woman living in a village. The grandmother of the village, with an important ritual role.

Zhalai: Jino blacksmith. They think that if blacksmiths are able to smelt iron is because the Goddess of the Blacksmiths allows them

Zhuoba. The eldest person of the main clan in the village. He occupies the highest ritual and political position in the village. His title means "mother of the village", and the sacred female drum used at all village sacrifices and festivals is stored in his house

Zhoule: The family-head in the primitive Jino long-houses. Under his leadership the long-house members worked together, lived together, worshipped together and shared among themselves.

Zhuosheng: Also zhouse. Father of the village. He is the oldest man in the second main clan of the village. Sometimes this title has a different name.